Simon Starling – Nachbau

Sponsored by RWE 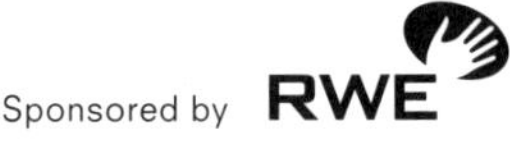

Simon Starling – Nachbau
Museum Folkwang, Essen
Volume II

Contents

The photographs by Simon Starling reproduced on the following pages
are copies of photographs originally made by Albert Renger-Patzsch in
the 1920's and the 1930's which today can be found in the Photography
Collection of the Museum Folkwang. From 1929 until World War II Albert
Renger-Patzsch was responsible for the photographic documentation
of both the permanent collection and its presentation within the
museum's buildings, in which his studio was also housed.

The Museum Folkwang was founded by Karl Ernst Osthaus in Hagen in
1902. After his early death in 1921 large parts of his collection were
moved to Essen. From 1929 they were exhibited in the new Museum
Folkwang in Essen, which was comprised of two existing buildings, the
Goldschmidt villas, as well as a significant extension by the architect
Eduard Körner on the Folkwang's present site. The photographs by
Renger-Patzsch were taken in Körner's museum extension. In 1944/45
the villas and Körner's building were destroyed by bombing. Today the
so-called "Altbau" (old building) of the Museum Folkwang, which was
inaugurated in 1960, stands in their place.

Simon Starling's copies of Albert Renger-Patzsch's original installation
photographs where made in a purpose built reconstruction of part of
Körner's museum building for the project "Nachbau". The reconstruction
and re-hang of this part of the original Essen museum was realised
in the 1983 extension to the museum, the "Neubau", and marks the
imminent demolition of that building.

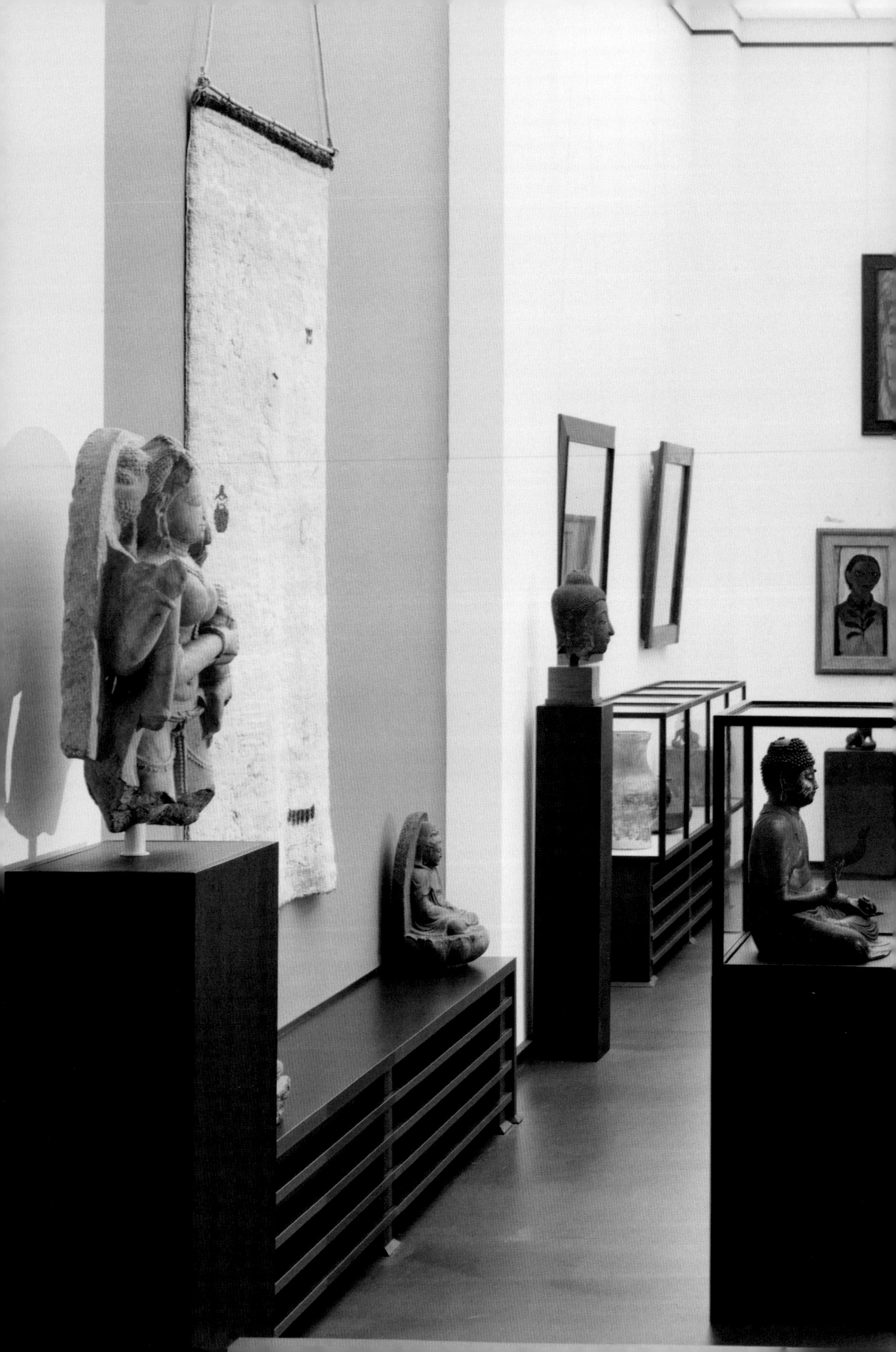

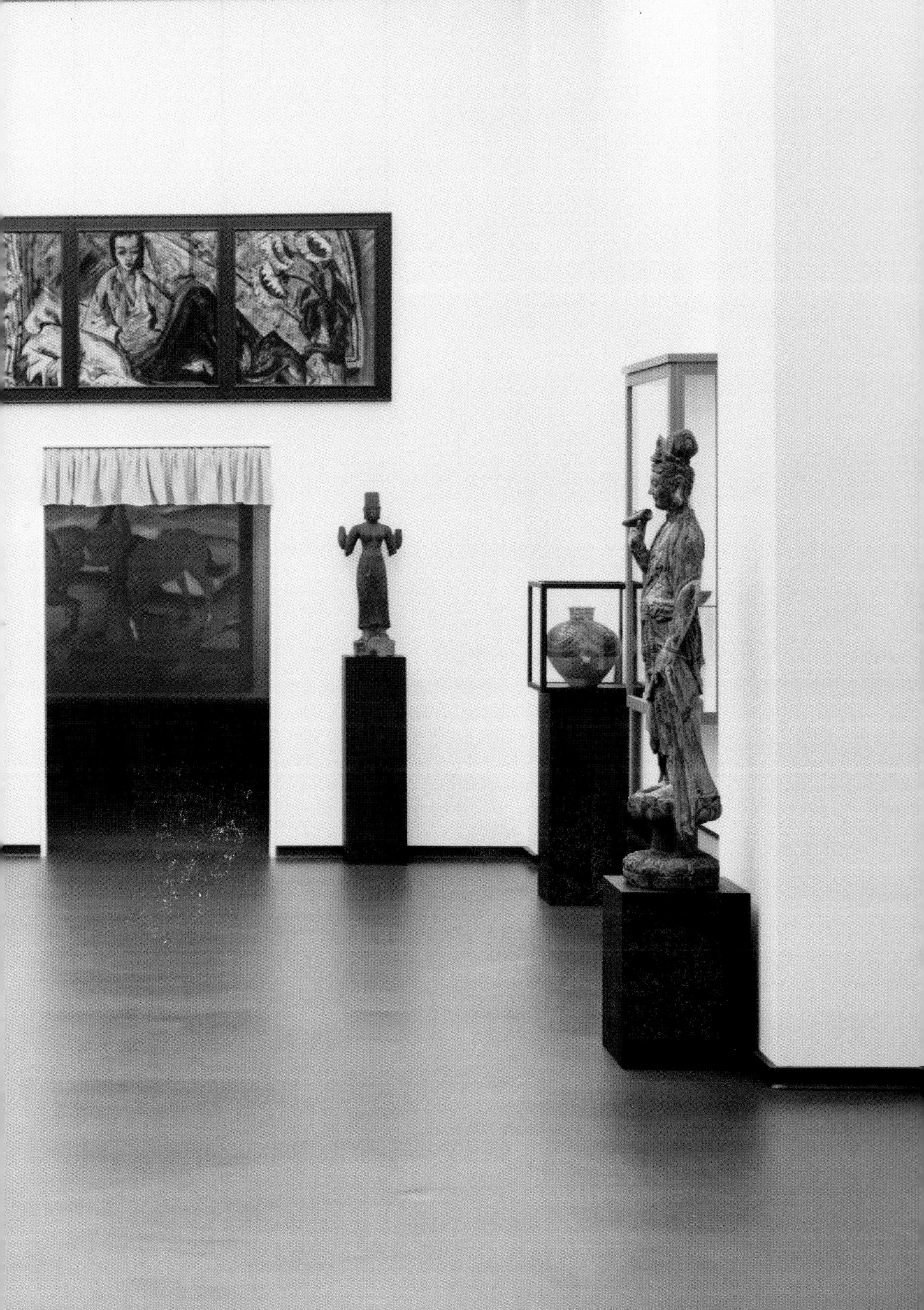

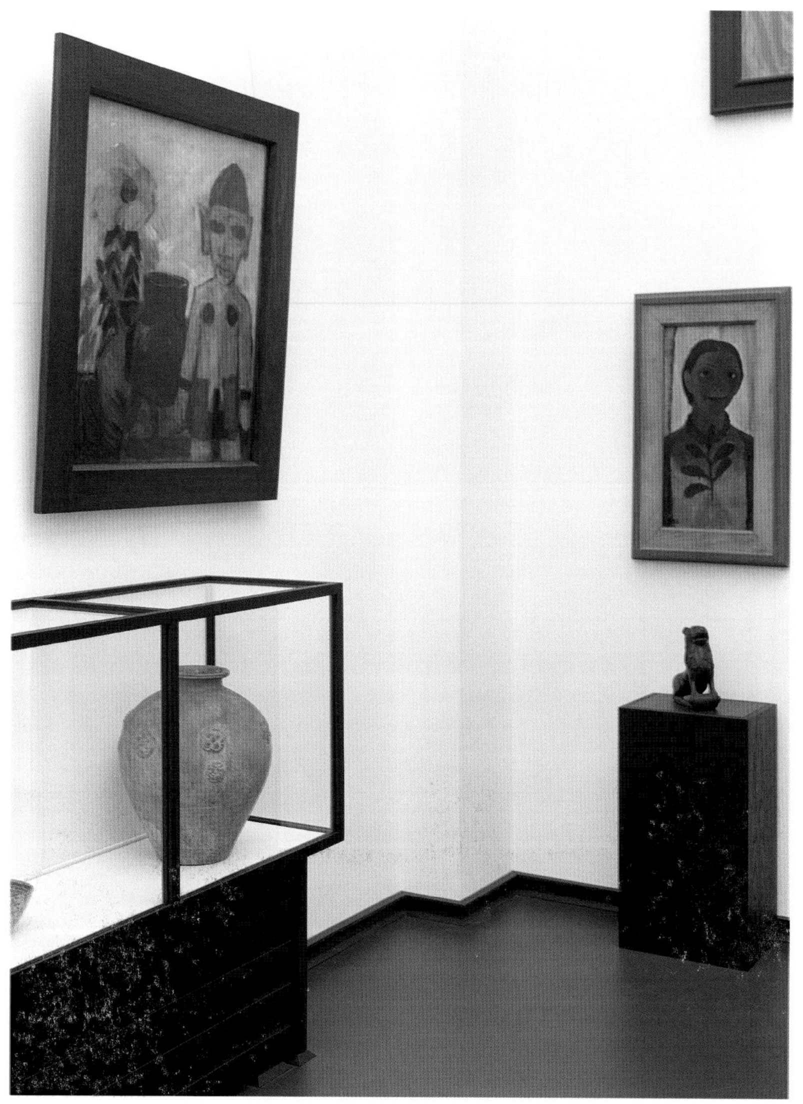

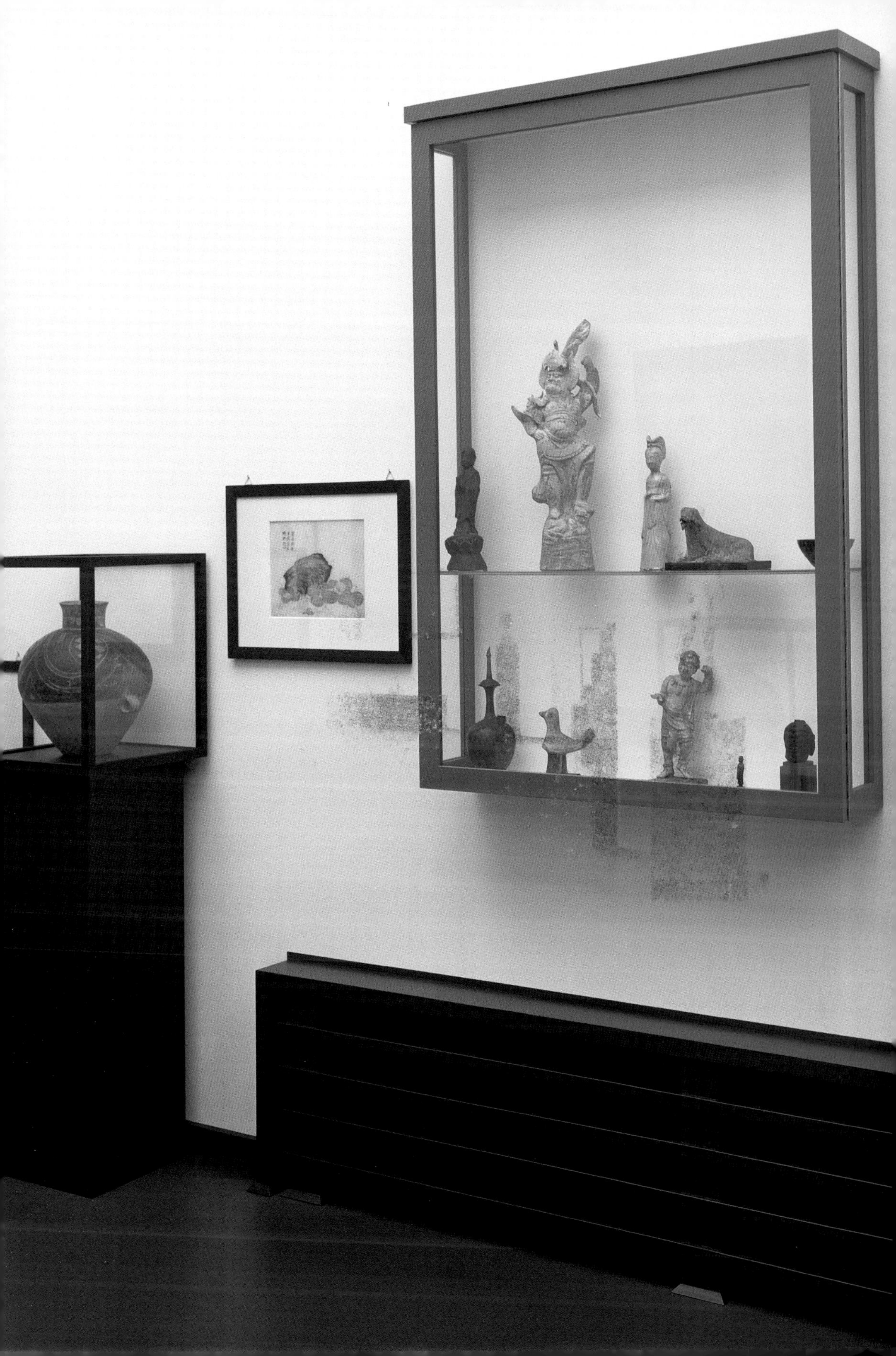

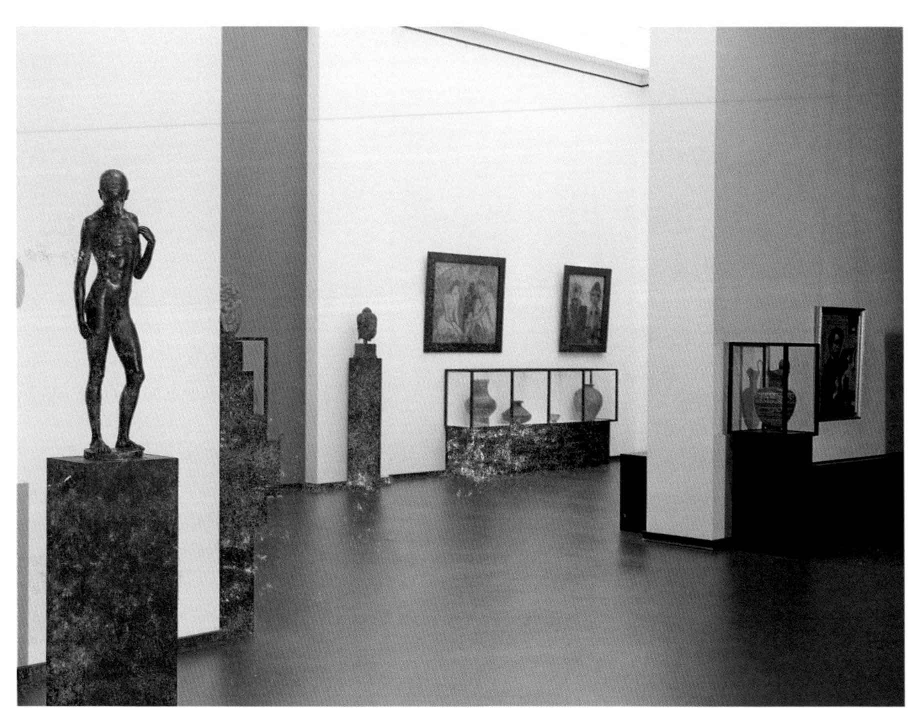

Bruno Haas

Fate, writes Hegel, "does not restore their world to us along with the works of antique art... but only the veiled recollection of that actual world. Our act of enjoyment of them is therefore ... an external activity – the wiping-off of some drops of rain or specks of dust from these fruits, so to speak – one which erects an intimate scaffolding of the dead elements of their outward existence, the language, the historical circumstances, etc. in place of the inner elements of the ethical life which environed, created, and inspired them. And all this we do, not in order to enter into their very life, but only to possess an idea of them in our imagination."[1] The home of a work of art that has lost its world is the museum. The artwork's *weltverlust* (loss-of-world) is indicated by the glass showcase. It separates the viewer from the work, in order to conserve it for posterity, though it is, in fact, evidence of a rupture: the rupture that separates our own world from the world in which the work of art was created. The only way for visitors to enter that world is by a leap of imagination that brings them into proximity to the Bodhisattva (fig. pp. 24–25), in other words, by entering, in the mind's eye, the proper space of the artwork itself as represented by the glass showcase. Certainly since Hegel's time, the museum has been defined by this rupture. It is the place where those objects are kept that have lost their world, insofar as they have lost that world. What is more, since Hegel's time, and probably much earlier still, art has also been created specifically and expressly for the museum. This is a bewildering situation – a situation made possible by that same *weltverlust* and by the fact that a work of art, in this loss-of-world, still means something to us, so that the loss is, in itself, a positive aspect of our own world. It is only under these circumstances that the relationship between art and life can become a matter for contemplation and reflection. The question as to whether art and life are separate or interrelated, and whether 'art and life' can be reunited after their alleged separation, also addresses the issue of the museum as a place not only for objects that have lost their world, but also for objects that have been created for a place that is a repositoryof objects that have lost their world.

What, then, is a museum? And why are works of art still kept, even when they have lost their world? In the text cited above, Hegel compares the fate of art-without-a-world to a young girl offering these artworks to us like fruits. And "...just as the girl who offers us the plucked fruits is more than the Nature which directly provides them – the Nature diversified into their conditions and elements, the tree, air, light and so on – because she sums all this up in a higher mode, in the gleam of her self-conscious eye and in the gesture with which she offers them, so, too, the Spirit of the Fate that presents us with those works of art is more than the ethical life and the actual world of that nation...", the nation referred to here being the Ancient Greeks.[2] In other words, the very fact that an artwork that has been uprooted from the world in which it was created actually imbues it with something more; the artwork is a thing that retains and acquires meaning even when uprooted. The possibility of *weltverlust* – of continuing to be, after having lost its world, and thus entering another world – this possibility belongs to the very essence of the artwork, just as, to our own world belongs the museum,
the possibility of receiving works of art that have lost their world.

The museum is the home of this homelessness. Within the structure of the museum as an institution, this function constitutes the unreflected, unsalvaged moment that has both underpinned and undermined the museum since its inception. Let us try to grasp what this means by way of example of a work belonging to the Museum Folkwang. The work in question once hung in the museum's former premises, was later sold off as 'degenerate art', only to be re-acquired at a later date for the collection, and is now presented in a reconstructed setting based on a photograph by Albert Renger-Patzsch in which it can be clearly seen. It is Paula Modersohn-Becker's Self-Portrait. We will later ask what this painting is doing here.

Even in Hegel's day, as we have seen, there was such a thing as art created specifically and exclusively for display in a museum setting. This applies not only to academic art, but also to the non-academic, sometimes even 'avant-gardist' art of the nineteenth and twentieth centuries. Consider, for instance, a Salon painter like Ary Scheffer who spent the last years of his life painting a *Temptation of Christ* that was

46

intended to be a perfect work of art. Or take a programmatic work such as Gauguin's *Where Do We Come From?...*, which the artist's friends wanted to donate to the Musée du Luxembourg in Paris for no other reason than the fact that it simply did not belong in the context of a private collection.[3] But as soon as works of art specifically address the museum, the function of the museum changes and so, too, does the function and concept of art. It is only where artworks that have lost their world are displayed for their own sakes that art can be formulated as 'absolute art', i.e. as an absolute value, as something that exists only in and for itself. Of course, this absoluteness and autonomy merely indicates a new form of belonging to the world; from here on, art has an autonomous place in 'life'. The notion of *l'art pour l'art* is merely a later, more specific version of a structure that was already well established by the early nineteenth century and had even been addressed by authors like Schelling and Hegel.

This form of absoluteness, then, defines the artwork as a value. Which, in the first instance, means nothing more than the fact that the artwork itself is 'valid' – that it 'counts' as a work of art. But what does that mean: being a work of art? Under the circumstances now emerging, it means nothing other than being a *valid* work of art. In other words, its value is no longer just one attribute of the work, but its very essence and defining characteristic – its *definiens*. It is no coincidence that it is only since the nineteenth century that there has been an ongoing debate about whether something is indeed art because it possesses certain inner values.

Needless to say, there were debates before that about how to paint, write or compose music properly. But these debates always centred on the actual execution of something whose existence as a painting, a piece of music or a poem was not contested. They did not question whether something was 'art' in the first place. Indeed, this abstract notion of 'art' has only been with us since the nineteenth century. The works of, say, Marcel Duchamp, prompt the question: "Yes, but is it art?" The response involves demonstrating that such things are accomplished and valid artworks, that they have a value.[4] The 'absolute' art created for a museum setting is thus defined by its value. Not that

47

the notion of works of art having a value is in itself a new idea – even the Ancients were willing to pay very high prices for works by certain masters, as Pliny reports. What is new, however, is that this value has become the *definiens* of art. This thoroughly modern position is at the foundation of the specifically modern fetish character of the artwork. The institution serves to determine the validity of artistic values in the dual sense of responding to values (by publicly purchasing and conserving works known to be valuable, i. e., valid) or creating values (by wielding its authority to consecrate hitherto unknown works). It goes without saying that this value can be translated into economic value. The fetish character of the modern work of art is thus to be understood in the Marxist sense of the fetish character of the commodity, albeit with the subtle difference that, in the case of the artwork, this value simultaneously functions as its *definiens*. The mere 'value' of the artwork is the empty signifier that constitutes the Being-Art of art, no matter how that value may otherwise be justified. The museum, however, is the abode of that abstract value. This (new) function of the museum does not replace its older function as the place of art that has lost its world,

it merely grows rampant upon it.

The performative character of the artwork in the specifically modern and contemporary sense is based on this function. According to various definitions, all of them rooted in the broader context of conceptual art (e. g. Donald Judd, Joseph Kosuth, Sol LeWitt), a work of art becomes a work of art by being declared as such. The term 'work of art' is in itself meaningless, but once an object has been declared to be a 'work of art', it triggers a 'work of sense' by which it is decided whether it is valid, i. e. truly a work of art. Hence, the work reproduces (or not, as the case may be) its character as art, namely its abstract value, through something that is not in itself an abstract value. The term 'work of art' thus takes on a performative function. Yet the institution is nothing but the possibility of that performative act itself, for which reason theoreticians such as George Dickie, Arthur Coleman Danto, Jean-Marie Scheffer and Yves Michaud have all tried in their various ways to understand art as a function of the institution. In doing so, they have followed impulses which, as we have seen, emanate from art itself and

which are therefore best analysed within this art.

This puts the artist in a singular position in relation to his or her own work. In a certain regard, we have to say that such a work has no author at all, in much the same way that Roland Barthes hailed the 'death' of the author back in 1968.[5] Let us take a look at how this phenomenon impacts on the work of Simon Starling. –

We have stated that institutionally and performatively defined works have, in a certain sense, no author at all. But only in a certain sense, for in another sense they do indeed necessarily have an author. They have an author insofar as they have to be signed, which is to say, insofar as someone has to declare them to be art and take responsibility for them. This situation is strange enough in itself, given that there are important works of art with no identifiable author, and for which the aspect of signature and authorial responsibility evidently play no role. Take, for example, the pyramids of Egypt or many a masterpiece of Romanesque architecture. Within the scope of the performative concept of art elucidated here, however, the signature is a necessary aspect. On the one hand, it is merely a formality, a meaningless precondition of the artwork, which, once it has asserted itself as art, now has to prove its real ability to function as a good, i.e. valuable, work of art. In short, it has to prove it is art. In this respect, it is irrelevant who signs the work as long as it is signed at all. On the other hand, the work of art has to be truly valid, which means that a community of recipients must be persuaded of its value, take an interest in it and believe in it. But it is the artist who has to believe in this most of all, and to prove it through personal commitment. Only such commitment lends the signature the necessary 'value' and *gravitas*. And so, inversely, the name of the artist is taken very personally. It seems that, fundamentally, both these aspects of the signature play a role in all the art practices that are in any way related to the institutional concept of art.

However, such performatively and institutionally defined art has no author in structural terms. We can see this in the work of Simon Starling. There is a historical context here that has simply been reappraised or, rather, just presented: the partial reconstruction of a building designed by architect Eduard Körner and destroyed in the war; works of art, some of them no longer in their place because they were sold off as 'degenerate art' – in other words, traces of history; then a major photographer, Albert Renger-Patzsch, whose photographs were used as the basis for the reconstruction and whose view of the works is particularly interesting within the scope of a project addressing the institution of the museum, the reception of art and such like. In addition we have the particularly well-designed new building of 1960 and next to it the extension of 1983 (in which Starling's work is installed). The latter is due for demolition this year, to make way for a new building. By its very presence in the Museum Folkwang this project raises questions about the future of the museum and of art. All these elements speak for themselves and are given a voice by the very fact that they have been gathered together here. At the same time, it is of little importance at which point the artist actually oversees or controls the parameters involved. On the contrary, in structural terms, these parameters go beyond his horizons; they are historical facts. In this respect, the author departs from the position, which Roland Barthes held to be imaginary anyway, of authorial identity that can assume responsibility for the work as a matter of personal intention. "The text is a tissue of quotations drawn from the innumerable centres of culture. Similar to Bouvard and Pécuchet, those eternal copyists, at once sublime and comic and whose profound ridiculousness indicates precisely the truth of writing, the writer can only imitate a gesture that is always anterior, never original,"[6] writes Barthes, having already stated shortly before that, "it is language which speaks, not the author."[7] According to Barthes, then, the wholeness of the text no longer rests with the author, but with the reader, inasmuch as the reader is the one who decodes and articulates the text, and ultimately the one who analyses it structurally (in the sense of separating the different sources brought together in the text and relating them to one another). The author (*auctor*) loses his authority (*auctoritas*). In the same vein, Simon Starling does not make himself an author in the traditional sense, but functions instead as a reader, at the centre of a confluence of disparate utterances that he merely assembles, but that each speak for themselves. And yet, Starling also speaks for himself within this orchestration, in other words, he takes on authorial responsibility – or, more precisely, by dint of his signature, he accepts responsibility for the whole as a work of art.

His involvement in the whole, insofar as he has lost his *auctoritas*, becomes a significant *moment* of that same whole. Thus, grammatically, he presents himself to us essentially in the third person, as an example of life, elaborated in order to evidence something. This is the real life of Simon Starling as an individual who, within certain constraints, generates a 'story', a 'history', of which we can learn more or less through interviews and the like, but which is also chronicled significantly enough in the documentation of his work. This is where the artists' discourse as an autonomous contemporary text genre has its place. In the case of Simon Starling this 'story/history' is characterised by a particularly lucid approach to the problem of authorship. Indeed, in most of Starling's works, if not all, the author is actually multiplied by two.

The twofold appearance of the author is this: the author encounters another author who has played a traditional authorial role – in this case, Renger-Patzsch. But think of Starling's replicas of design objects (Josef Frank, Poul Henningsen), or more complex works in which, for example, he reconstructed the radiator of the Bisiluro racing car designed by Carlo Mollino for Le Mans in 1955, and fitted it to a red Fiat Panda which was then driven around the Turin ring road for 24 hours,[8] or in which 'Mr Jeanneret' (Le Corbusier) meets Mr Naujok, where the currently empty studio of Le Corbusier at Ste Baume (Provence) is located opposite the humble farmstead of Mr Naujok.[9] In his *Notes on the Buildings of Mr Naujok and Mr Jeanneret*, the historic elements brought together in the installation, at the centre of which stands the bicycle designed in 1897 by Mikael Pedersen, are quite literally linked by a *narrative*, i.e. by a text that tells of a fictitious meeting between the two men. The text is even annotated with historical background facts. The annotations are not written by the artist, which means that they no longer come under his *auctoritas* in the sense outlined above. Yet the text and accompanying photographs are treated with such attention to detail that they could quite easily stand on their own. – The author and his double are not on equal terms. The Other Author (as a rule this is a dead author such as Le Corbusier, Carlo Mollino or Charles Eames, though exceptions include, say, Chris Burden) has a particular prestige – that of the *auctoritas* on which traditional authorship is based. But the One Author (the artist Simon Starling) treats the Other Author

as precisely what he is: as a phantom. The phantom of the Other Author
is the basis of the borrowed (inactual) authorship of the One Author.
But it is this latter authorship alone that inaugurates the event and
validity (the 'value') of the whole as a work of art.

The author, it might be said, eludes us, transforming himself into a third
person, no longer addressing his audience directly, but transforming himself into a symptom – if, that is, a symptom is something through which
something else is manifested, 'co-inciding' with that something else.[10]

What factually occurs here within the *praxis* of a contemporary artist
has a background in historical theory. In fact, institutional art history
prepares the ground for this new situation in the reception of art, which,
needless to say, affects not only the author, but also the viewing public
and their attitudes and expectations. The erosion of the older claim to
autonomy goes hand in hand with the changing issues. By asking how
a community relates to a work of art – in other words, by objectifying
this relationship – we create a new kind of relationship to the artefact,
and that relationship, in turn, becomes an indirect one. From this indirect viewpoint, of course, the work does not look the same as it does
from the direct perspective of the 'naive' viewer. Whereas the 'naive'
viewer is captivated by the work, the institutional theoretician remains
'free', being able to bracket the direct appeal of the artefact by his or
her analytical approach, thereby evading it. So the critic evades the direct appeal of the artwork as a consequence of the logic of his argu-
ment. For as soon as the artwork's appeal is not related to oneself but
instead to a third person, such as the 'recipient', the 'author', the 'institution', etc., all of whom necessarily appear in the grammatical third
person, we are no longer dealing with the appeal of a work of art, di-
rected towards us. In this sense, then, the institutional critics' relativisation of the absolute claim of art is not the result, but the precondition,
of their work.[11] This introduces a new situation into the field of art:
far from being merely an 'objective' description of the structures already established in art, the relativisation of the absolute claim of art
functions as a performative instance in its own right. The situation it introduces also addresses the subject directly, like any other – the difference being that the subject it addresses directly is now affirmatively

defined by the performative institutional concept of art, which in turn has consequences for the position of the author, as we have sought to elucidate above with reference to Starling's work.

Simon Starling's work, too, can be described in terms of institutional theory. But in one respect, at least, it is a step ahead of the theory: it does not repress its performative contribution, but reveals it openly and lets it happen. Note how the works of art in the Museum Folkwang appear in his work as objects of indirect perception or *intentio obliqua.* We see, for instance, how Renger-Patzsch saw these works, but we do not directly see the works themselves. Of course, in seeing them as Renger-Patzsch saw them, we do not see them as he saw them at all, for, unlike us, he saw them directly. –

So what happens here? An event occurs.[12] All we shall say of this event is that it simply lets us 'be' in the midst of history and (hi)stories. All the circumstances involved participate in this event: the impending demolition of the 1983 building, the future of the new building, the past of the 1960s building, the chequered history of the collection, the gaze of the photographer. The event of the exhibition is but a fleeting moment – nothing final. The event has a time. Which time? A time other than everyday time, a time that has been detached from everyday time. The detached time in this event does not pass. It is a *number.* What is a number? Numbers play an important role in all of Simon Starling's work. Dates are given everywhere: for the Körner building, for the Bisiluro in the Turin work mentioned above, for Pedersen's bicycle. The number has nothing to do with the thing – even less than the name. Numbers are relative. But this is precisely why numbers tell us where we belong. However, we are the Where we are in, if Being (*Sein*) is the same as Being-There (*Da-sein*). Because the year 2007 has a number, it can remain the year it is, even in the future. If we could not count (*tell*) time, it would not pass and it would be still less able to remain the same. We *tell* time. This *telling* of time is produced specifically by a work of art that allows time to happen. It is 'art'. –

So far, we have detailed the stratification of the museum's various functions in order to describe a certain unremarkable event that occurs as

a co-event within the event of this exhibition. I do not know whether this event was 'intended' by Simon Starling, but that is of little consequence, inasmuch as he lays no claim to being an author with 'intentions'. However, the author of this text intends and hopes to enter into a dialogue with the work of the artist, by specifically naming and highlighting this co-event, that is, listening to its appeal and, in turn,
responding to it with a question.

The event consists quite simply in the fact that, in this installation, the Self-Portrait of Paula Modersohn-Becker is not hanging in its place.

The Self-Portrait of Paula Modersohn-Becker is an important work of art. We want to see in what way it belongs in the museum, i.e. in what way it is where it is. In order to find out, let us take a look at the picture itself.

This painting is a self-portrait. The face in the picture seems to look at us. It is up to us whether or not we respond to the question in this gaze. If we choose to do so, we enter the radius of the sitter's gaze and find ourselves drawn closer to the artwork. What kind of intimacy is this? – As soon as I enter the circle of this intimacy, I have the impression that the picture is enclosing me. I no longer just see something in front of me, but am also aware of something behind me, which, admittedly, I cannot see as long as it is behind me. I am surrounded by a warm, slightly broken olive green. This olive green is mirrored on the face of the sitter, in the shadows, on the nostrils, on the forehead. There, it is mixed at times with an orange hue. The green radiates with a warm and rather heavy inner light; we are in a room. This interior light is very different in nature from the pale blue light – daylight – that falls into the picture space from behind the sitter. A pale curtain covers the window in the room; the face is backlit and is touched by the weaker shimmer
of green that comes from behind me. Behind me is green.

But there is also a light rising from below, illuminating the face from beneath. This light is paler than the matt, shadowy green; it has a yellowish-red tinge. It is between me and the person in the picture. The picture receives these three lights, absorbs them, contains them. It is solidly constructed and drawn. The drawing is black. In places, for instance in the hair, the black alternates with brown, which lends the drawing a certain sculptural mass. What is more, the white that offsets this black/brown comes in all manner of shades, but is rarely pure. A secret place, of which we shall speak later, forms the centre of this structural framework: the grey of the left eye. This, then, is the framework in which the three lights are embedded. These three lights put me in a certain place, take me into the picture. They do this in a mysterious way that almost defies description. The green that envelops me is not just the colour of a reflection on the face, cast by a light that must, logically, be coming from behind me. For this colour also relates strangely to the ochre beige of the ground. Add to that the prussian blue, where it tends towards black, and these three colours form a family; they generate an atmospheric undercurrent in the picture into which the daylight pours through the blue curtain as an adventitious Other. Inasmuch as the green is behind me, with the ochre beige of the ground responding to it, it draws me into the intimacy of the picture. I enter the duration (*Dauer*) of its time. What is created by this duration into which I enter when I approach the picture, I shall call enduring (*Bedauer*). In its relationship to the ochre beige of the ground and the dark prussian blue,

the green is the enduring.

In the midst of this closeness to the picture, this intimacy, there burns a fire. The third light that illuminates the face from below, yellowish and actually red, burns in a place where the image has already broken off, framed by the two black stripes that vaguely suggest the sitter's dress. Here, at the lower left, are the initials PMB. This black-framed red fire is actually the main focus of the picture. Out of this fire rises the stalk of the camellia: two leaves touching on the right, three leaves hanging side by side on the left, one leaf in the middle, at the top. We begin to count them. What is a number? Why does the number rise from the fire, borne by a hand so lightly sketched that it is the most vulnerable and tender thing in the picture? The property of a number is that it situates without bearing even the slightest relation to the thing it situates. I can, for instance, be my parents' second son and thus forfeit all the privileges of the first-born. But there is nothing in my nature that

55

makes me the second. The number has nothing to do with us, but it situates us and thus becomes our fate. The branch in the hand of Paula Modersohn-Becker puts some numbers between us: two, three, but the last twig is hard to count, i. e. difficult to situate numerically. It holds the centre between two sides and should therefore be an uneven number, a 'masculine' number as the ancient arithmeticians called it,
but altogether there are exactly six.

Paula Modersohn-Becker's eyes each have a different expression. Her right eye is tired and resigned, as though it no longer sees anything, while her left eye is alert and seeing. The same with the ears. The right ear, turned slightly towards us, is like an empty, reddish-raw excoriation: deaf. But the left ear, barely visible because the head is turned away slightly, hears. Of course, both eyes and both ears belong to one and the same person; our description is exaggerated. And yet, there is within this person a duality, a division and it is strangely underlined by an inconspicuous stripe in the curtain, slightly to the right of centre,
just above the parting of her hair.

The right eye, as we have said, is as though it were blind. Now we put it to you that this blindness is aptly expressed in the German language by the fact that 'the eye' is neither a masculine nor a feminine noun, but neutral: *das* Auge. The left eye is seeing or, to use a common turn of phrase, it shines. We shall designate this shining eye by unconventionally using the feminine article: '*die* Auge'. This *feminine* eye is a shade of grey that does not occur anywhere else in the picture. The *neutral* eye, though it is also grey, is of a slightly browner hue. The colour grey is actually 'colourless', it is said. But this grey is strangely, ineffably luminous. This ineffable luminosity of grey is what I mean when I say '*die* Auge'. Αὐγή (feminine) is the Greek word for luminosity, such as the overwhelmingly radiant luminosity of the sun.

But what lies in the radiance of the self-aware eye and in the gesture
of overture? –

The mouth is red. What words would this person say if she opened her mouth? We do not know. Does she know it herself? Is this a person who knows what she wants? Perhaps not. Perhaps not, in the sense that her will does not always coincide with itself and with the circumstances. What this mouth would say might be a contradiction. There is an abeyance there. Is there not a discrepancy between the neutral eye (*das Auge*) and the feminine eye (*die Auge*)? This person does not have a *will* in the sense of wanting something clearly defined and therefore unequivocal, self-contained, an object. But she does possess a determination that goes beyond will; the determination to follow a path. This determination is silent. It speaks through the gentle blue abeyance of the background. The red of the mouth stands before the blue of the veil that divides the light of day from the 'fire'. This division opens up the space wherein the person is situated. Where something can be because there is an opening of space: this is what we call freedom. Therefore we shall call the pale blue drape before the window the veil of freedom.[13]

Let us hear at last what the mouth says: 'Guilty and not guilty. We are just as good or as bad as we are. There is little point in doctoring around on oneself. One should simply and directly follow one's path. I think I am by nature a good person and if I occasionally do something bad, well, that's natural as well.'

Paula Modersohn-Becker really did write those words – in a letter to her sister Milly Rohland-Becker, dated 12 August 1906, presumably a few months before she painted the self-portrait.[14] At the time, she was living in Paris, where she enthusiastically embraced the latest developments in painting. At the time, she was considering separating from her artist husband, the much older Otto Modersohn, who nonetheless supported her financially during this crisis, paying her accommodation and expenses in Paris. Paula's friends and family could barely comprehend her attitude to her generous and patient husband. But she just went on painting.

What is a picture as a work of art? Where does it belong? What is a museum? We address these questions to Paula Modersohn-Becker's Self-Portrait. This painting draws me into the enduring (*Bedauer*), into the proximity of the sitter. In such proximity, it holds out to me the veil that opens the freedom wherein that person is. The picture shows, it presents all this; it is pure self-presenting that withholds nothing. It is, after all, only a picture, with no reverse side; it doesn't hide. The picture is a pure gift.

What does the picture give? It gives by showing, revealing, presenting, the existence of the woman, her freedom. But it is only a picture. There is no Being (*Sein*) in the picture, only Appearance (*Schein*). So this picture is not a real gift, in that the painter does not give 'her self'. But in fact every real gift, according to Lacan, involves giving what one does not have: Nonbeing.[15] Just as, inversely, according to Schelling, To Be itself is Nonbeing in its eminent sense. But To Be is a sense. The gift, therefore, is essentially an image; for the image is the thing inasmuch as it is not, the thing as the pure self-giving of sense.

Who does the picture give itself to? – Where does the picture belong? Nobody can claim to be the specific addressee of this picture. Nobody could claim that, even if the painter had actually had a certain person in mind (of which, in this case, we know nothing). Nor is it possible to think of any one particular addressee for such a work of art, thereby excluding others. For this picture is a self-presentation, which, in showing itself at all, *speaks*. But it shows itself only out of the abyss of sense that belongs originally to all, for all, in turn, belong to it, out of which they all are what they are.

In the Körner Building this self-portrait hung opposite the stairway to the second floor, to the left of the passage leading into the sequence of galleries that were grouped around the inner courtyard (fig. pp. 24–26). On closer inspection of the floor plan, we realise that Körner had envisioned a specific type of building. Beyond the imposing entrance with its *cour d'honneur* there was a narrow entrance passage-way leading past the ticket office. Then came a spacious reception room with windows overlooking the cour d'honneur. To the left of this was the entrance to the inner sanctum of the museum, where the Old German Imperial Eagle was exhibited with a late medieval statue of the Madonna centerstaged in the background, in what might be

58

described as the 'apse' of the room, or, in the words of the architect, Eduard Körner, 'the affectionate architectural embrace of the individual artwork'.[16] Straight ahead, however, a few steps led to the fountain known as the *Minnebrunnen*, standing in a rotunda designed especially for it. Only after passing through these initiatory rooms did visitors finally enter the 'private' area of the building, which began with the setting photographed here. Then came a sequence of fairly large rooms, followed by smaller ones and, finally, the second floor. What is meant by describing the character of the building as 'private' might be phrased as follows: this house feels lived-in. Except that the person living in it is no longer there. The objects are 'tastefully' arranged, connections have been made, the Bodhisattva has a central position as 'head of the household'. But Paula Modersohn-Becker (like the oriental female statue, the servant opposite her) has been banished to the back of the house, as befits a woman's place (fig. pp. 24–25). The fact that a phallic object[17] has been erected at precisely the place that is marked as the site of the 'fire' in the painting, is a lapse that does little to help us gain a better understanding of the picture, but nevertheless contributes a great deal to the symptomatic content of this presentation of the museum's collection. In the older photo, the photographer shows this object protruding directly over the showcase containing the meditating Bodhisattva, but in a later photograph, taken from a lower vantage point, it is cropped by the upper edge of the same showcase. By the way they are arranged, the artworks become symbols of the functions of the building, with which they in themselves have nothing to do. For instance, Paula Modersohn-Becker's painting clearly has a tense relationship to the function it embodies, deadened, as a symbol. This, too, is the reason why the statues are placed on plinths[18] and in showcases: so that they can adopt that symbolic function as spaceless, abstract *signifiants*. However, it is crucial to the museum that the inhabitant of the building, who is at the imagined centre of those symbolic functions, is no longer there: he is deceased. The museum, in other words, is a grave. In the case of the Museum Folkwang, the deceased has a name: Karl Ernst Osthaus. He appears as a form of alienation of the visitor and the object. Our relationship to the objects is tempered by the fact that the late recipient was able to appreciate them in a way the paying public can not, namely as their legal owner. Paying

59

the entrance fee and walking through the narrow corridor from the
ticket office that interrupts the transition from the cour d'honneur to
the entrance hall sets the seal on this situation.

If we now turn to the photographs that Renger-Patzsch made of the
collection, we can easily divide them into two categories: those that
show the works in situ in the Körner Building, and those that show individual works in some unspecified location. Among them there are also
some aesthetically highly appealing photographs of ancient vases and
objects, some grouped together, others alone, that tell of a different
attitude. Here, the photographer has succeeded in capturing the sim-
plicity of their material existence and, in doing so, has achieved a sense
of closeness and intimacy that would be difficult for any museum visitor
to obtain. The view is, in principle, the gaze of the collector himself, of
the one who lives among these objects.[19] The photographer brings this
gaze to the public and, in doing so, proves the objects' (purported)
content of mystery and truth, which they can no longer elaborate in the
mummified state of their presentation in the museum setting. The simple
fact that the aesthetic value of these objects is, in a certain respect,
manifested only in the photograph, is in itself an obvious indication of
the degree to which value is imaginary in the most literal sense of
the word, in that it has become a function of the image. Not that this
alters the fact that the objects themselves might be true works of art
which, on display here, are not in their rightful place. But what is their
'rightful place'? – It is the museum, though not inasmuch as the museum
gives them a home, but, rather, inasmuch as they give themselves a
home within the museum.

1 GFW Hegel, *Phenomenology of the Spirit*, tr. A. V. Miller, ed. J. N. Findlay, OUP, London 1977, pp. 455–456.

2 Ibid., p. 456.

3 Ary Scheffer, *Temptation of Christ*, 1851–57, Paris, Louvre; Paul Gauguin, *Where do we come from? What are we? Where are we going?*, 1897, Boston, Museum of Fine Arts.

4 Thierry de Duve, ed., *The Definitive Unlimited Duchamp*, MIT Press, 1993.

5 Roland Barthes, 'La mort de l'auteur', in *Œuvres complètes*, vol. 2, 1966–1973, ed. Eric Marty, Paris, 1994, pp. 491–495. English: Roland Barthes, "The Death of the Author", in *Image–Music–Text*, tr. Stephen Heath, London, 1977, pp. 142–148.

6 Ibid., p. 146.

7 Ibid., p. 143.

8 Exhibition at the Franco Noero gallery in Turin, May 2006.

9 *Simon Starling*, ex. cat., Villa Arson, Nice and Städtische Ausstellungshalle am Haverkamp, Münster, Münster / Nice 2003.

10 Jean-Jacques Rousseau begins his *Confessions* (1770) with the words "I have resolved on an enterprise which has no precedent, and which, once complete, will have no imitator. My purpose is to display to my kind a portrait in every way true to nature, and the man I shall portray will be myself." (Rousseau, *Confessions*, tr. JM Cohen, London, 1953, p. 17) In what may well be the very first known instance of such a literary device being used, Rousseau – even when he speaks in the first person singular on his own behalf, as he does throughout – writes as though he were a third person standing before a court of law or a panel of assessors. In short, he speaks of himself as a symptom, insofar as his text is intended to *show* who he is without him actually *saying* so directly himself.

11 See, for example, Jean-Marie Scheffer, who seems intent on challenging the entire canon of what he calls speculative art theory (*L'art de l'âge moderne. L'esthétique et la philosophie de l'art du XVIIIe siècle à nos jours*, Paris, 1992) and Yves Michaud, *La crise de l'art contemporain: utopie, démocratie et comédie*, Paris, 1997.

12 Daniel Kurjakovic has described some of the means by which Starling undertakes the event. See 'Hide and Seek in Simon Starling's Scenario', in *Simon Starling: Cuttings*, ex. cat. Kunstmuseum Basel (Museum für Gegenwartskunst) and Power Plant Toronto, Basel, 2005, pp. C26–C36.

13 "Freiheit ist das lichtend Verbergende, in dessen Lichtung jener Schleier weht, der das Wesende aller Wahrheit verhüllt und den Schleier als den verhüllenden erscheinen läßt." Martin Heidegger, 'Die Frage nach der Technik', in *Vorträge und Aufsätze*, Stuttgart 2004 (1954), p. 29. English: "Freedom is that which conceals in a way that opens to light, in whose clearing there shimmers that veil that covers what comes to presence of all truth and lets the veil appear as what veils." Martin Heidegger, *The Question Concerning Technology, and Other Essays*, tr. William Lovitt, Harper Row, New York, 1977, p. 25.

14 "Schuld und Nichtschuld. Man ist eben so gut oder so schlecht wie man ist. Das Herumdoktern an sich hat wenig Zweck. Man gehe gerade und einfach seinen Weg. Ich halte mich für gut von Natur und sollte ich dann und wann etwas Schlechtes tun, so ist das auch natürlich." *Paula Modersohn-Becker in Briefen und Tagebüchern*, eds. Günter Busch and Liselotte von Reinken, Frankfurt a. M., 1979, p. 456.

15 "Ce qui est aimé dans l'objet, c'est ce dont il manque – on ne donne que ce qu'on n'a pas." Jacques Lacan, *Le séminaire, livre IV*, ed. Jacques-Alain Miller, Paris, 1994, p. 151.

16 Cited in *Essener Allgemeine Zeitung*, 5 May 1929.

17 Listed in the inventory as 'Lion, early Asian, bronze, Inv. K. 536'.

18 It is under these circumstances that the 'problem' of the plinth as addressed by artists such as Manzoni or Rückriem originates in the first place.

19 Osthaus himself opened his collection to the public and saw the founding of a museum as an important social duty. The Hagen museum building that originally housed his collection is worthy of analysis in its own right, but suffice it to say here that it also has the character of a private home.

Simon Starling

1967	Born 30 May in Epsom, England.
1980	Built first home-darkroom.
1987–90	Studied Photography at Trent Polytechnic, Nottingham.
1990–92	Studied Fine Art at Glasgow School of Art, Glasgow and realised *Museum Piece* a site-specific installation in the Mackintosh Museum with fellow student Paul Maquire.
1990–96	Worked extensively as a photographer for a number of Scottish museums and art galleries.
1993–96	Served as committee member at Transmission Gallery, Glasgow.
1995	Had first solo exhibition at the Showroom Gallery, London, for which he reconstructed part of the London exhibition space in Glasgow to use as a studio.
1997	Built a small fishing boat in Marseille from a museum display case from the National Museum of Scotland, Edinburgh [*Blue Boat Black*]. Made a chair out of a bicycle and a bicycle out of a chair [*Work, Made-ready* Kunsthalle Bern].
1998	Flew a radio-controlled aeroplane over the Museum of Modern Art at Heidi, Melbourne [*Le Jardin Suspendu*].
2000	Produced *Pleçnik, Union* for Manifesta in Ljubljana, Solvenia by reconstructing a broken glass lamp and bottle from fragments found in the park outside the Moderna Galerija.
2003	Installed *Island for Weeds* (Prototype) in Palazzo Levi on the Grand Canal as part of Zenomap, Scotland's contribution to the Venice Biennale.
2004	Became Professor of Fine Arts at the Hochschule für Bildende Künste, Städelschule, Frankfurt.
2005	Made unrealised proposal to exchange two 2m diameter sections of the wall from the 1st and the 3rd floors of the Museum für Gegenwartskunst, Basel. Awarded the Turner Prize, Tate Gallery, London.
2006	Exhibited *Wilhelm Noack oHG* at Neugerriemschneider, Berlin.
2007	Projected a 35mm film-loop of a single silver particle from a photographic image of the Atomium at Wiels, Centre for Contemporary Art, Brussels [*Particle Projection* (Loop)].

Albert Renger-Patzsch

Born in Würzburg in 1897. 1909 made first photographic attempts. Encouraged by Waldemar Osthaus, the youngest son of Karl Ernst Osthaus, he went to Hagen in 1921. There he took over responsibility for the photographic archive of the Folkwang publishing company managed by Ernst Fuhrmann. Renger-Patzsch started to take photographs in European museums for books in the series *Kultur der Erde* (Culture of the World), published by Fuhrmann. After stays in Darmstadt and Bad Harzburg settled in Essen in 1929. Photographed for the Museum Folkwang, where he kept his studio until the museum's destruction in 1944. 1946 moved to Wamel on the lake Möhnesee, where he died in 1966.

Bruno Haas

Born in 1967. Studied Art History and Philosophy in Bonn, Freiburg, Paris and Rome. Publications on the philosophy of German Idealism, on methodology ("deictic-functional analysis") and on art history from the Renaissance to the present. Maître de Conférences at the Sorbonne, Paris 1.

Simon Starling – Nachbau

Gefördert durch 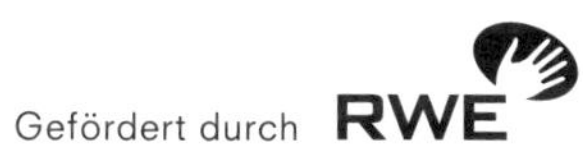 RWE

Simon Starling – Nachbau
Museum Folkwang, Essen
Volume I

Inhalt

Die auf den folgenden Seiten abgebildeten Fotografien von Albert
Renger-Patzsch entstanden in den 20er und 30er Jahren und sind Teil
eines größeren Konvoluts, das sich heute in der Fotografischen Sammlung des Museum Folkwang befindet. Renger-Patzsch besorgte von
1929 bis zum 2. Weltkrieg die fotografische Dokumentation der Be-
stände und ihrer Präsentation in den Räumen des Museums, in dem er
auch sein Atelier hatte.

Das Museum Folkwang wurde 1902 von Karl Ernst Osthaus in Hagen
gegründet. Nach seinem frühen Tod 1921 gelangten große Teile seiner
Sammlung nach Essen. Sie waren hier seit 1929 im neuen Museum Folkwang ausgestellt; dieses umfasste die beiden Goldschmidt-Villen sowie
den bedeutenden Erweiterungsbau von Eduard Körner am heutigen
Standort. In Körners Erweiterungsbau entstanden die Aufnahmen von
Renger-Patzsch. Villen und Körner-Bau wurden 1944/45 durch Bomben
zerstört. An ihrer Stelle steht heute der sogenannte Altbau des Museum
Folkwang, der 1960 eingeweiht wurde.

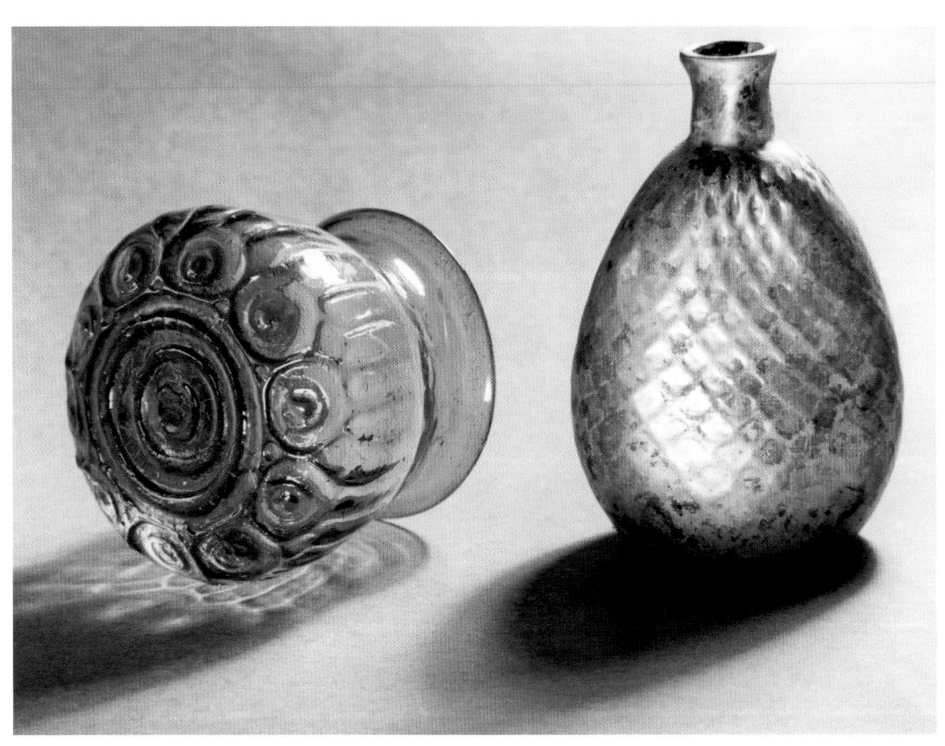

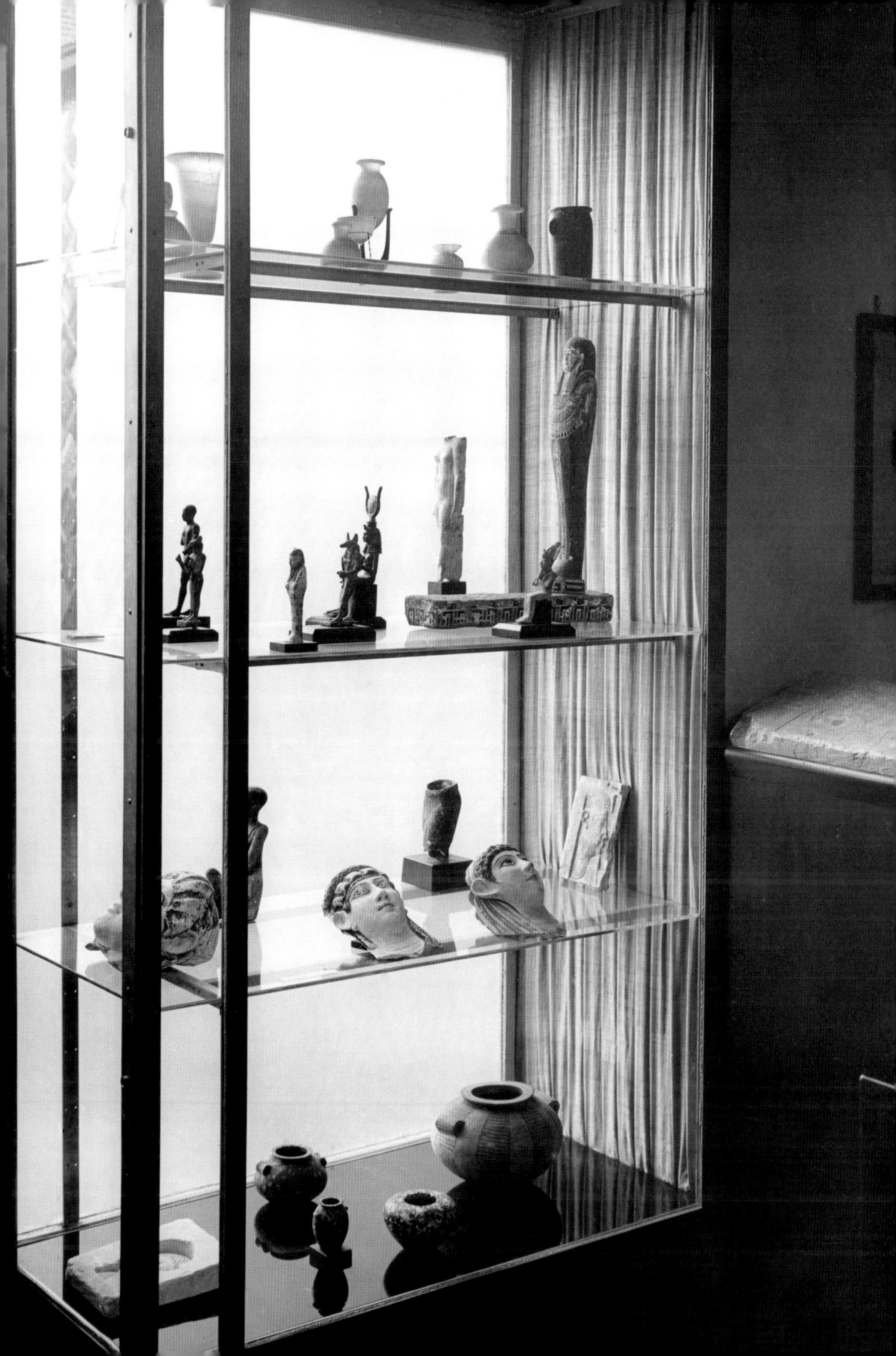

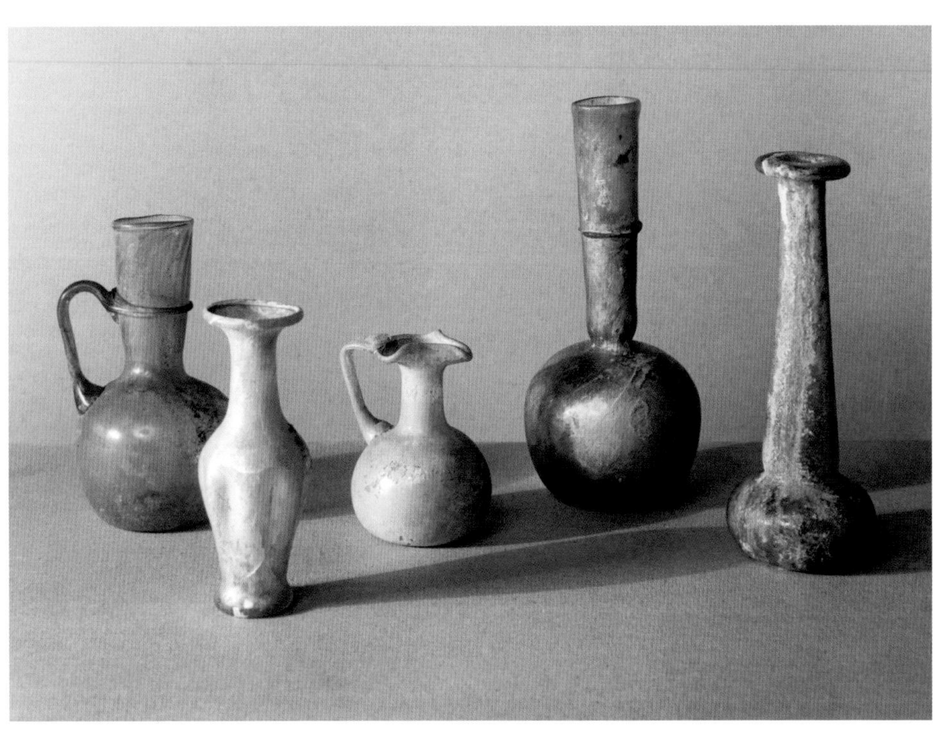

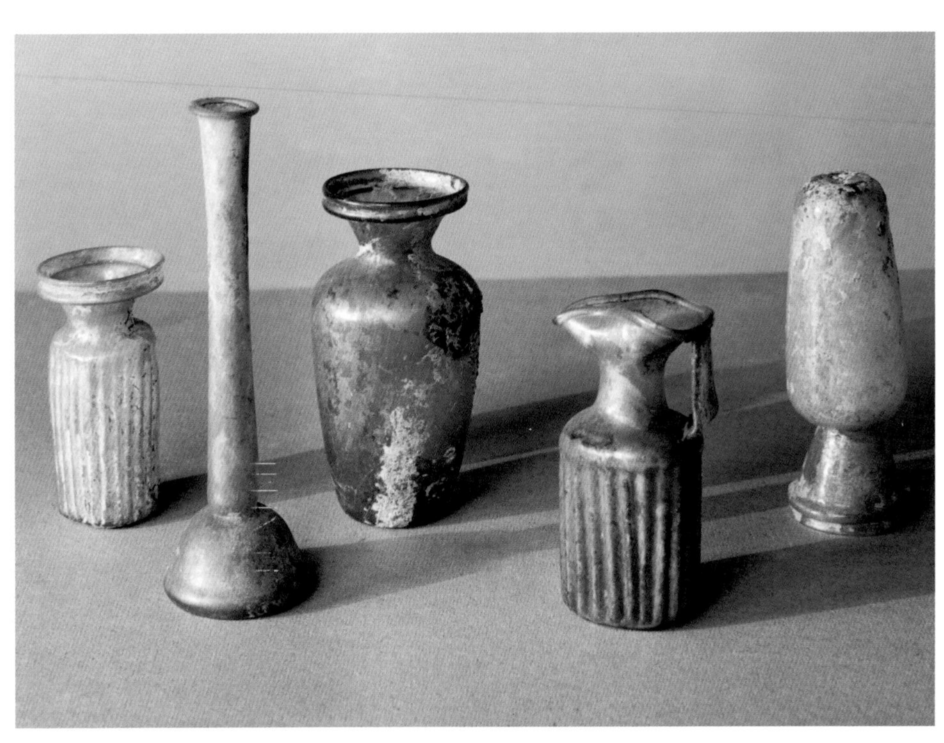

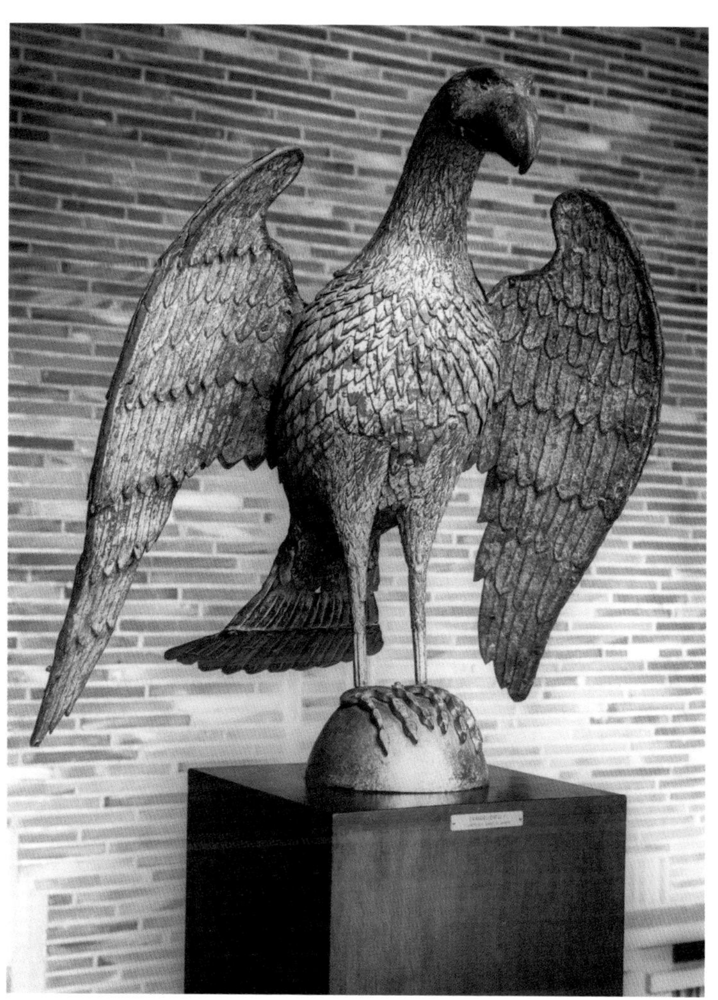

14

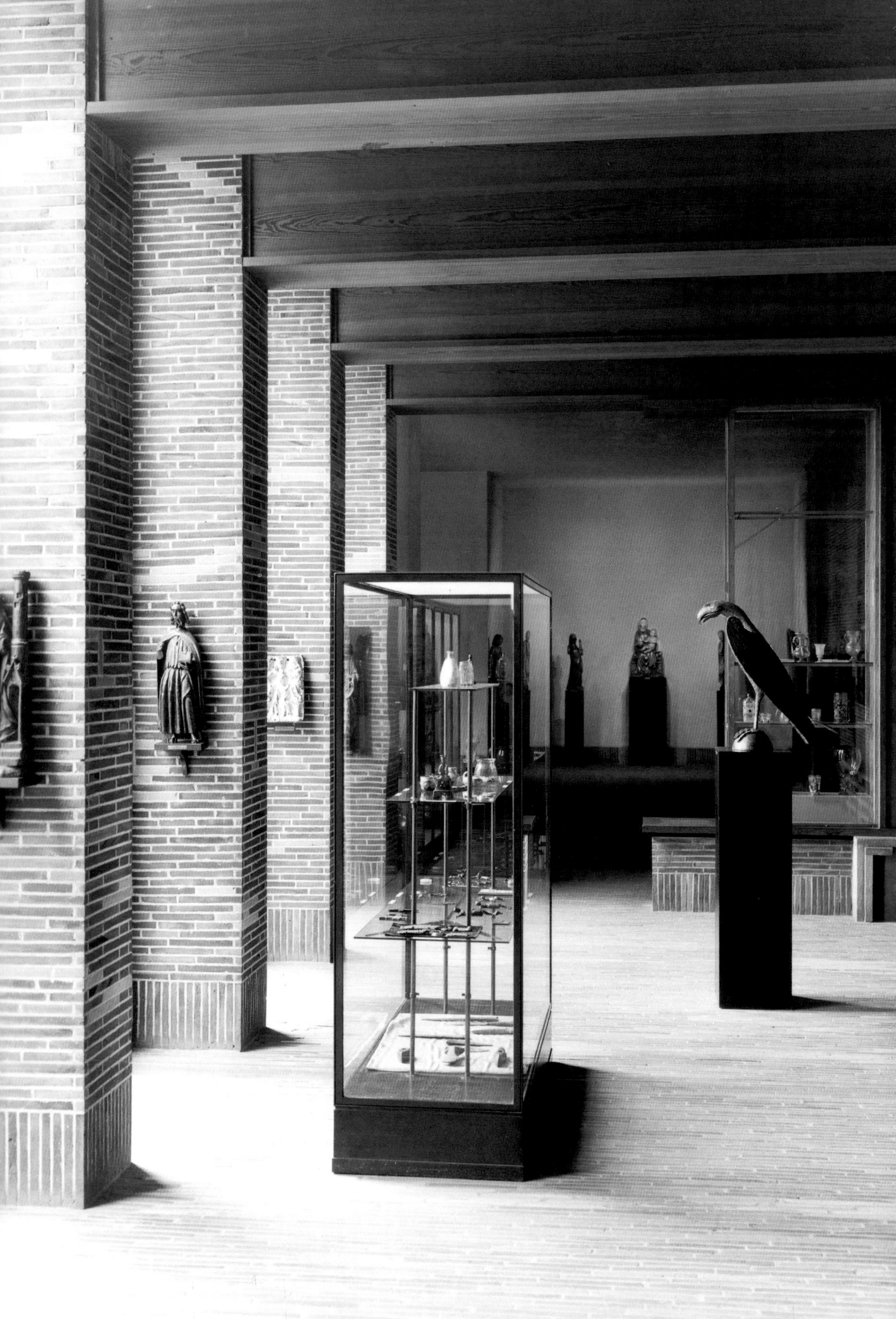

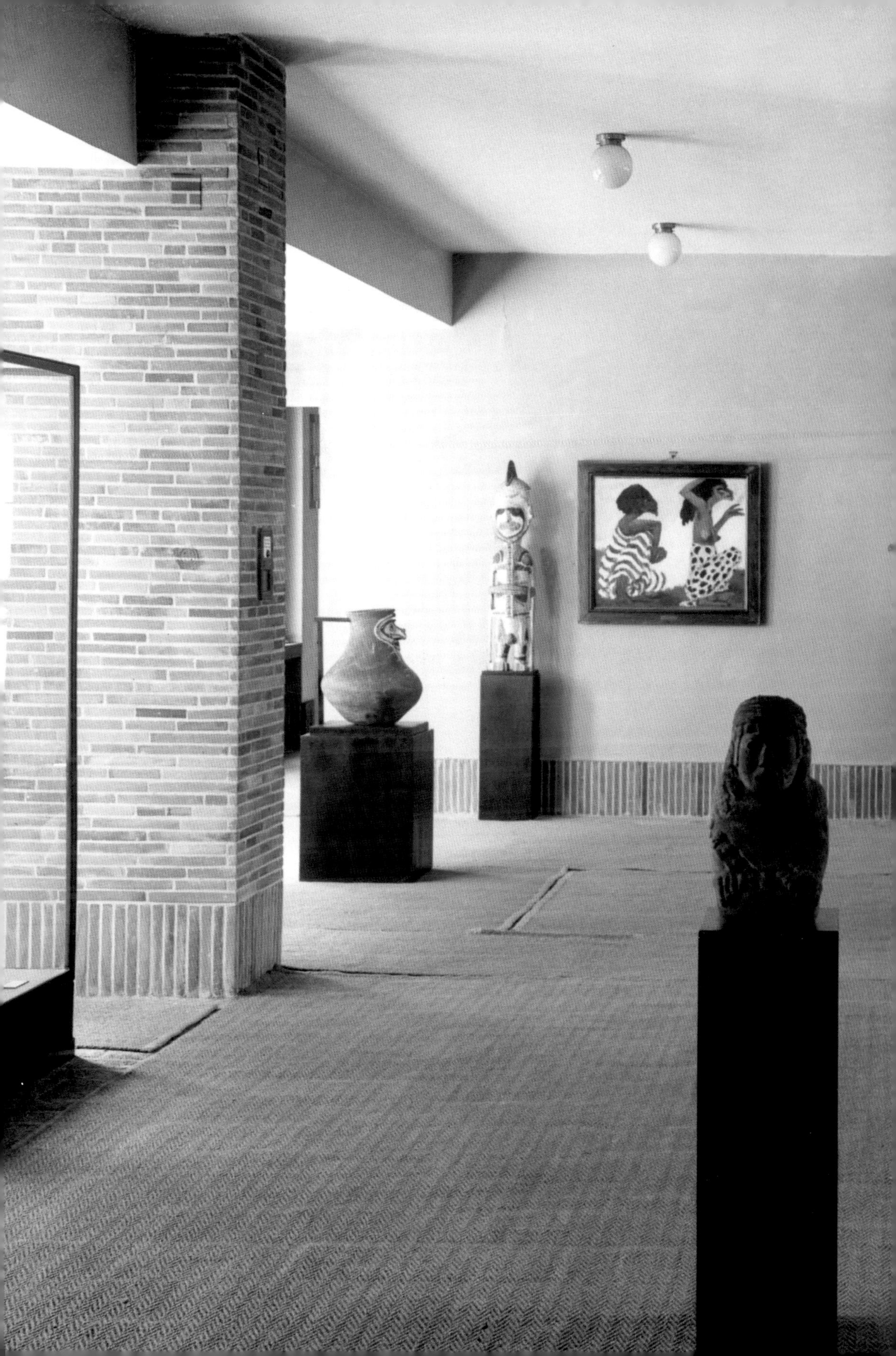

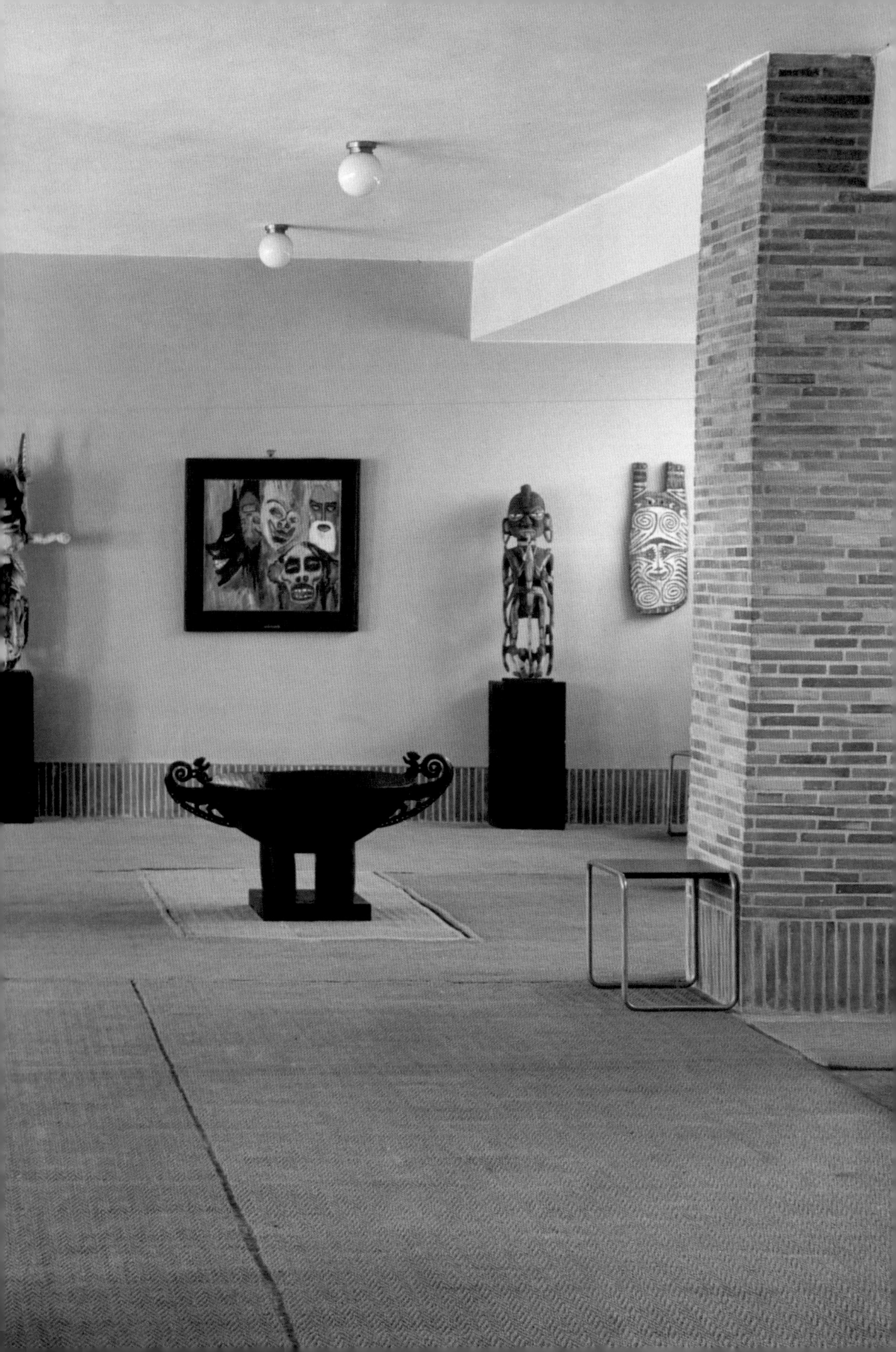

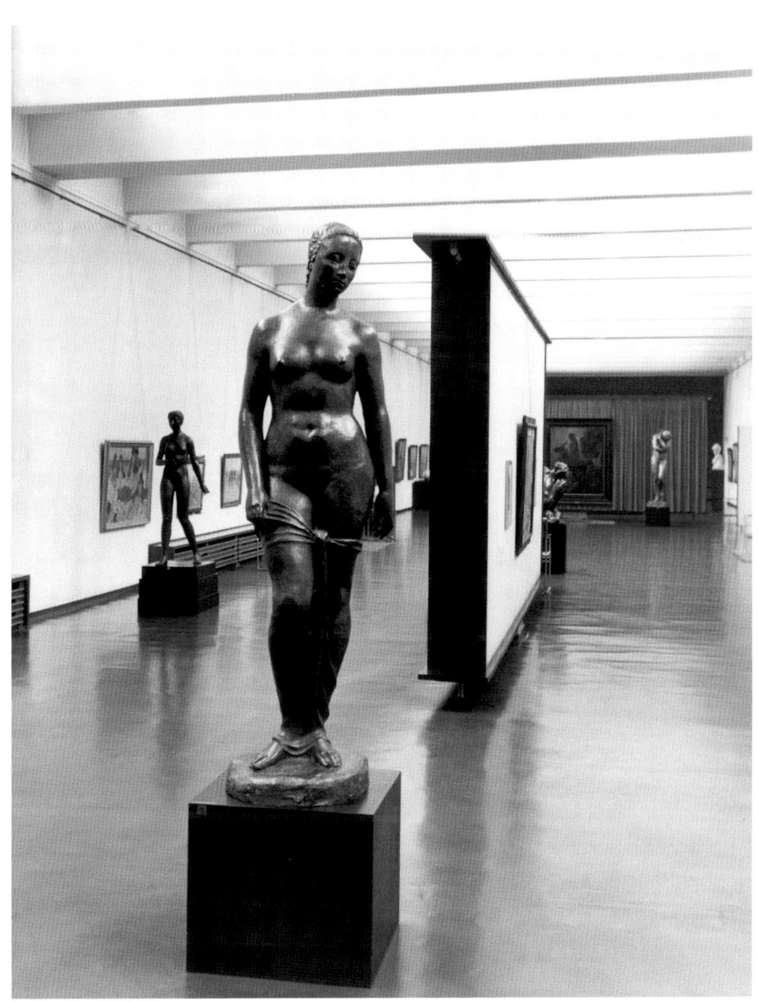

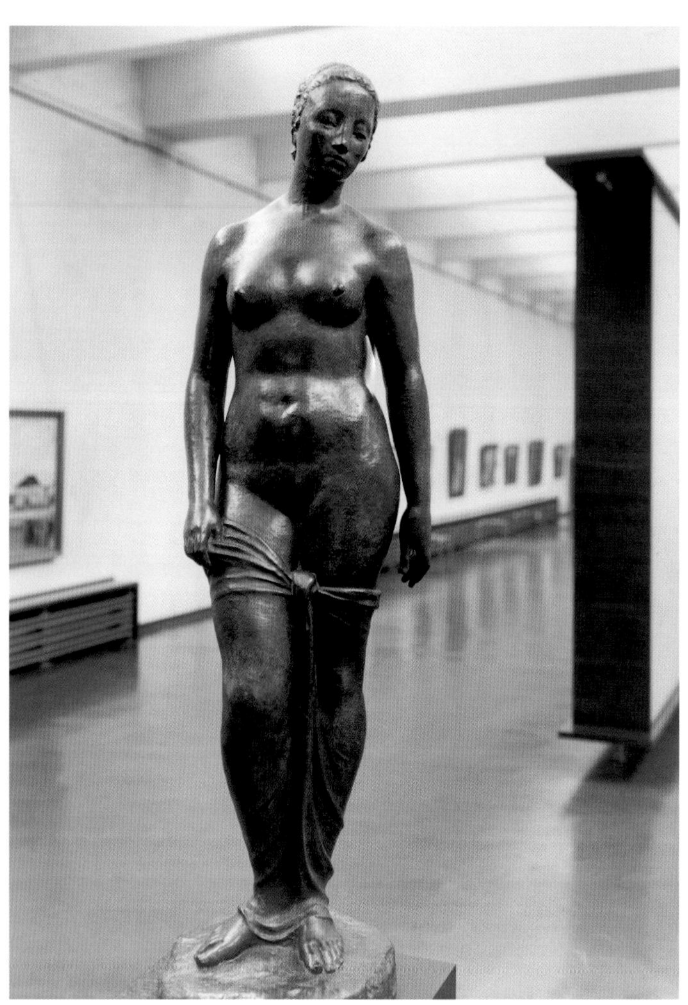

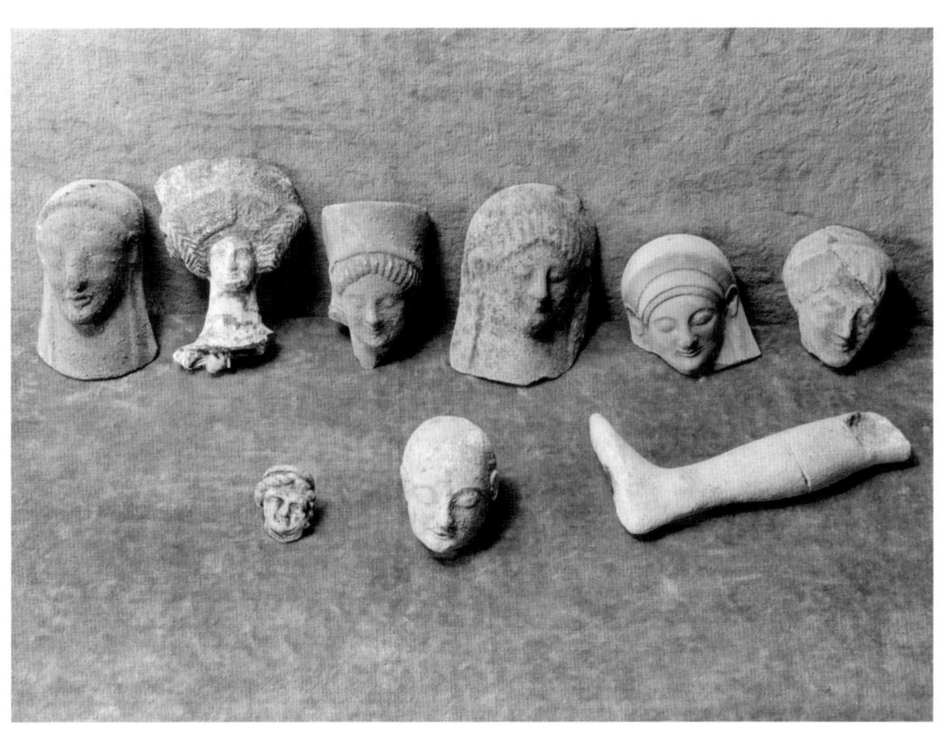

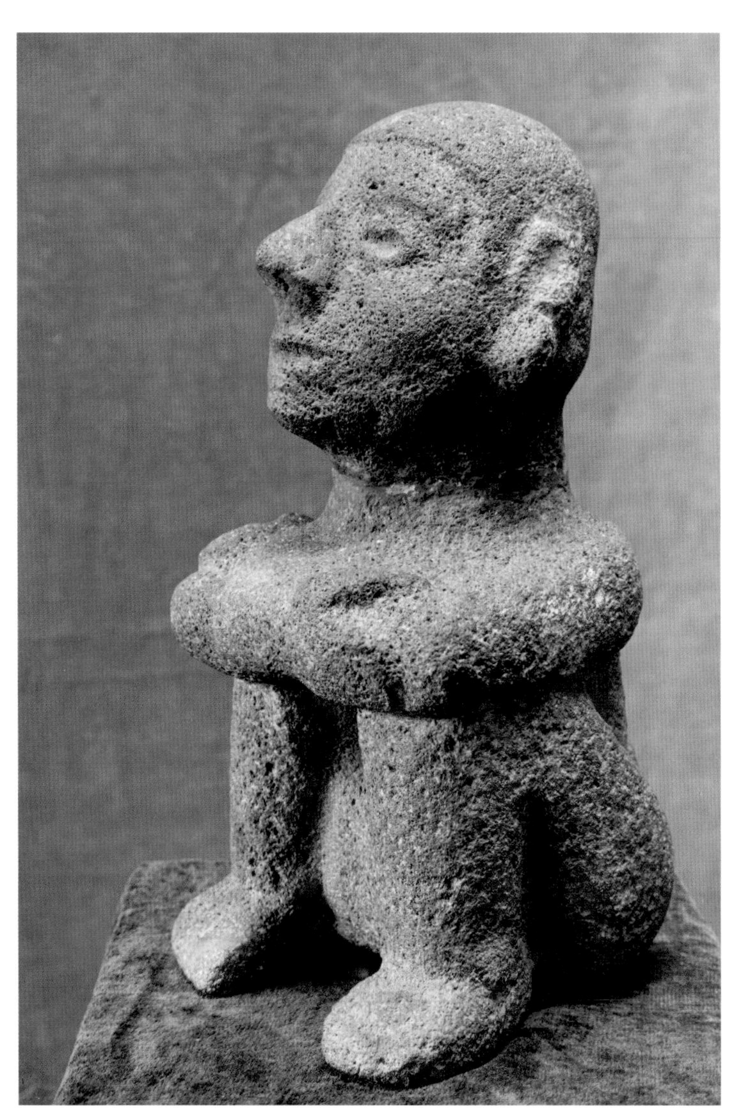

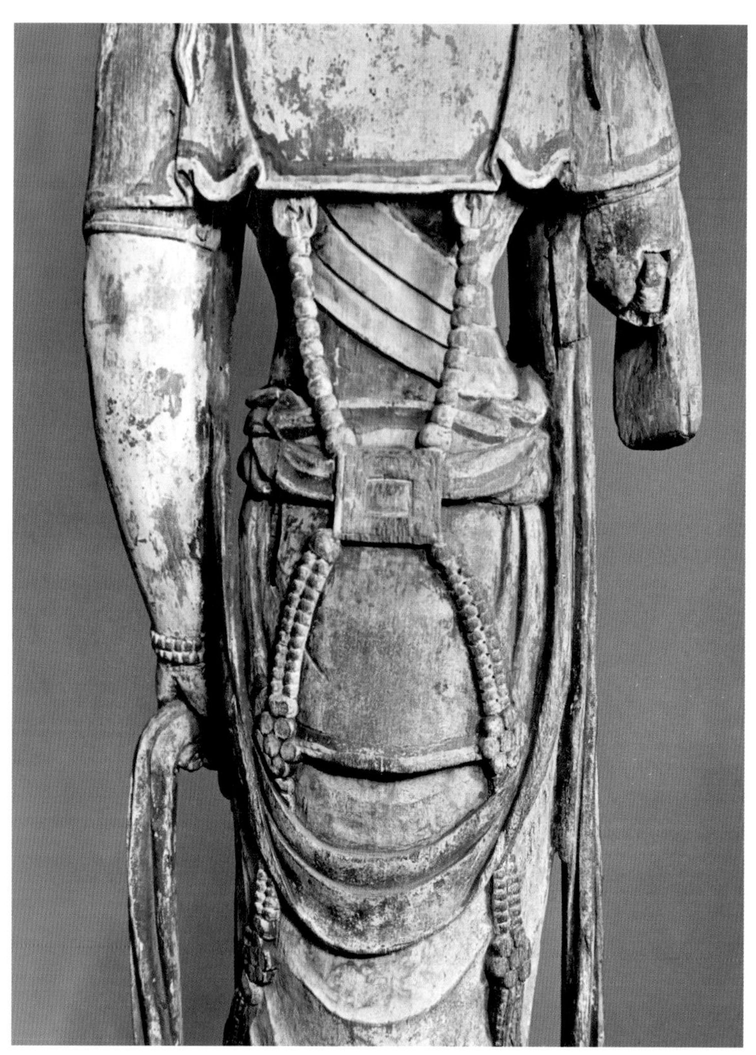

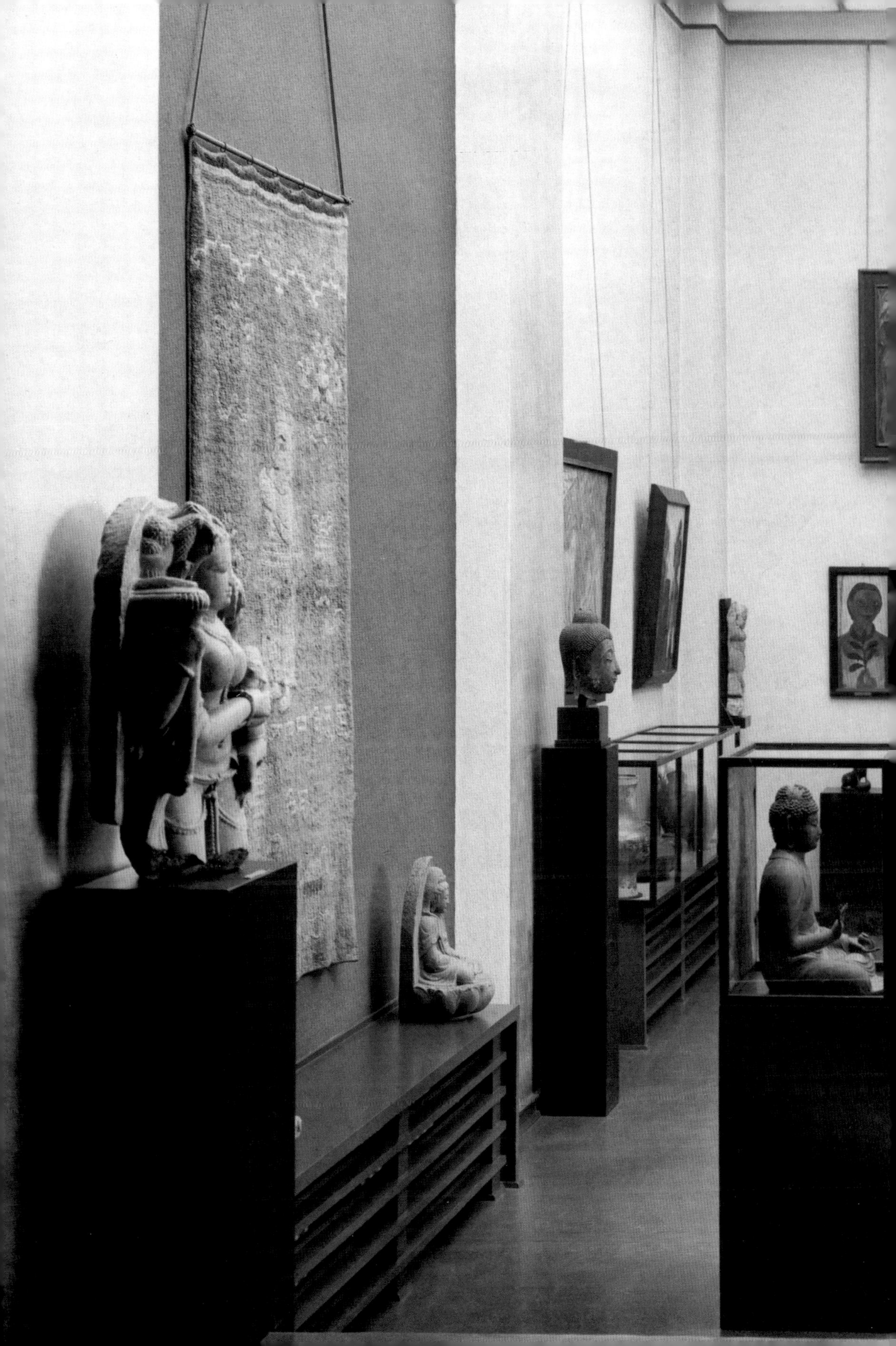

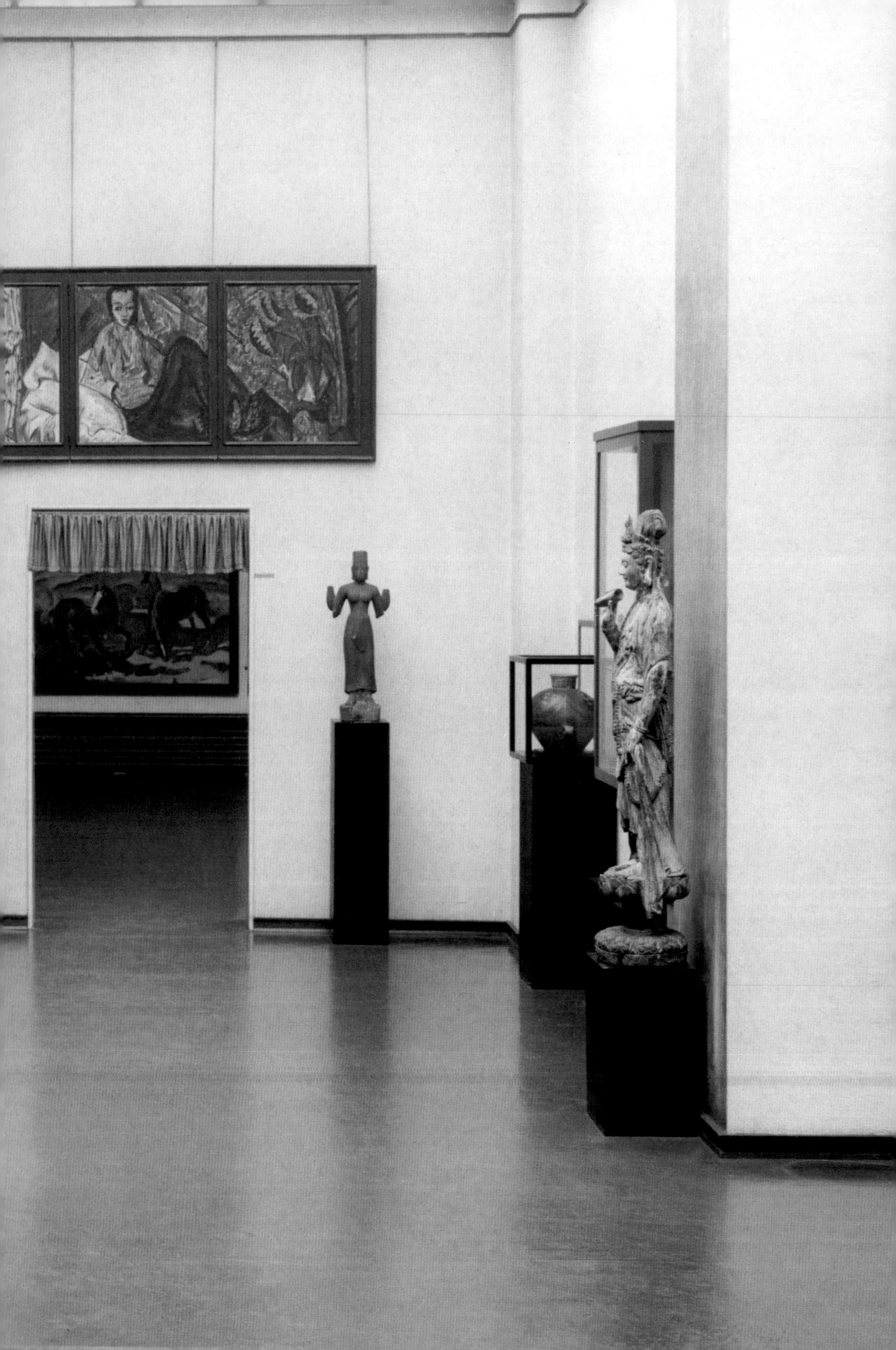

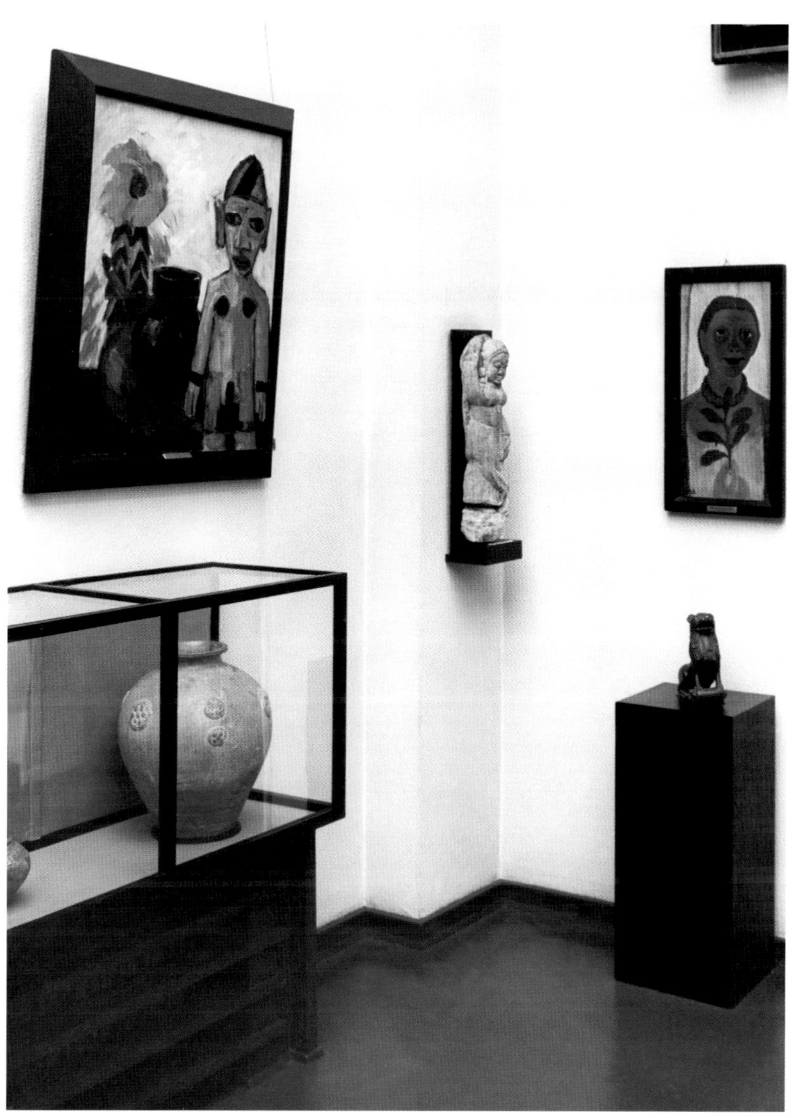

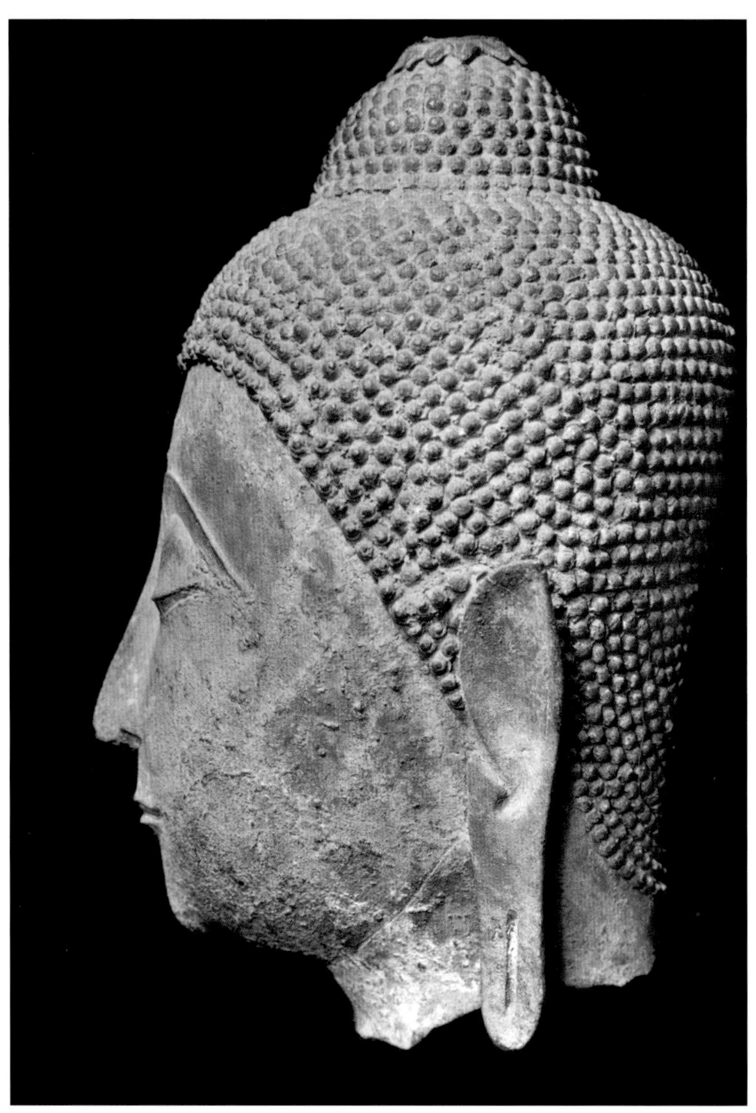

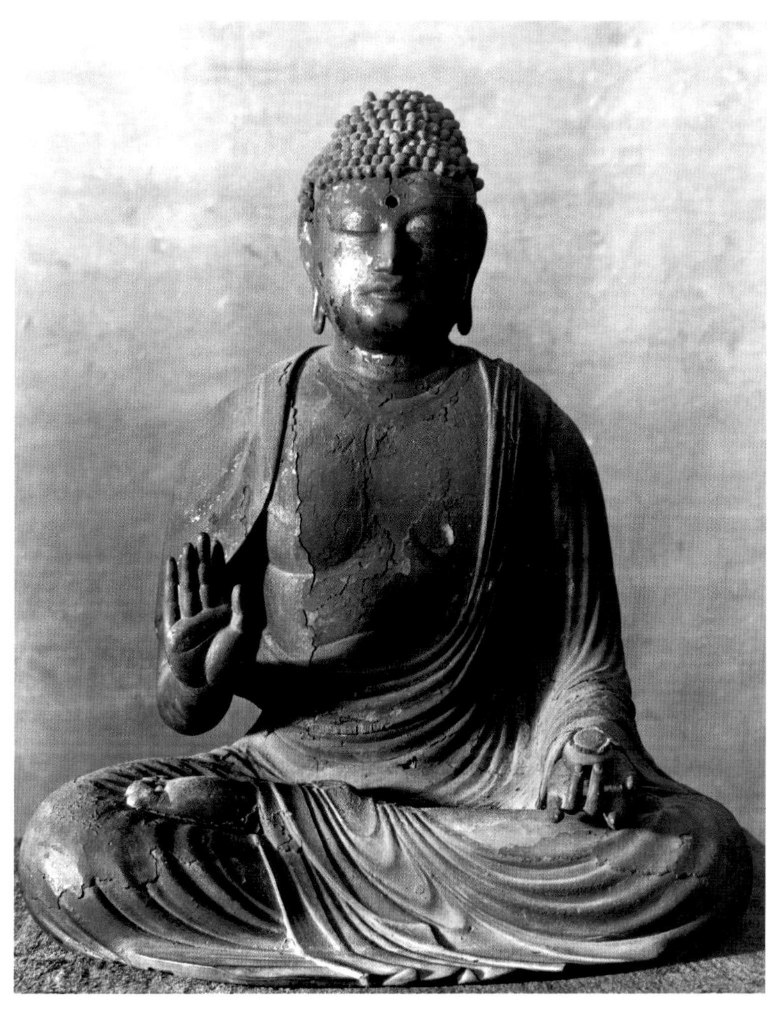

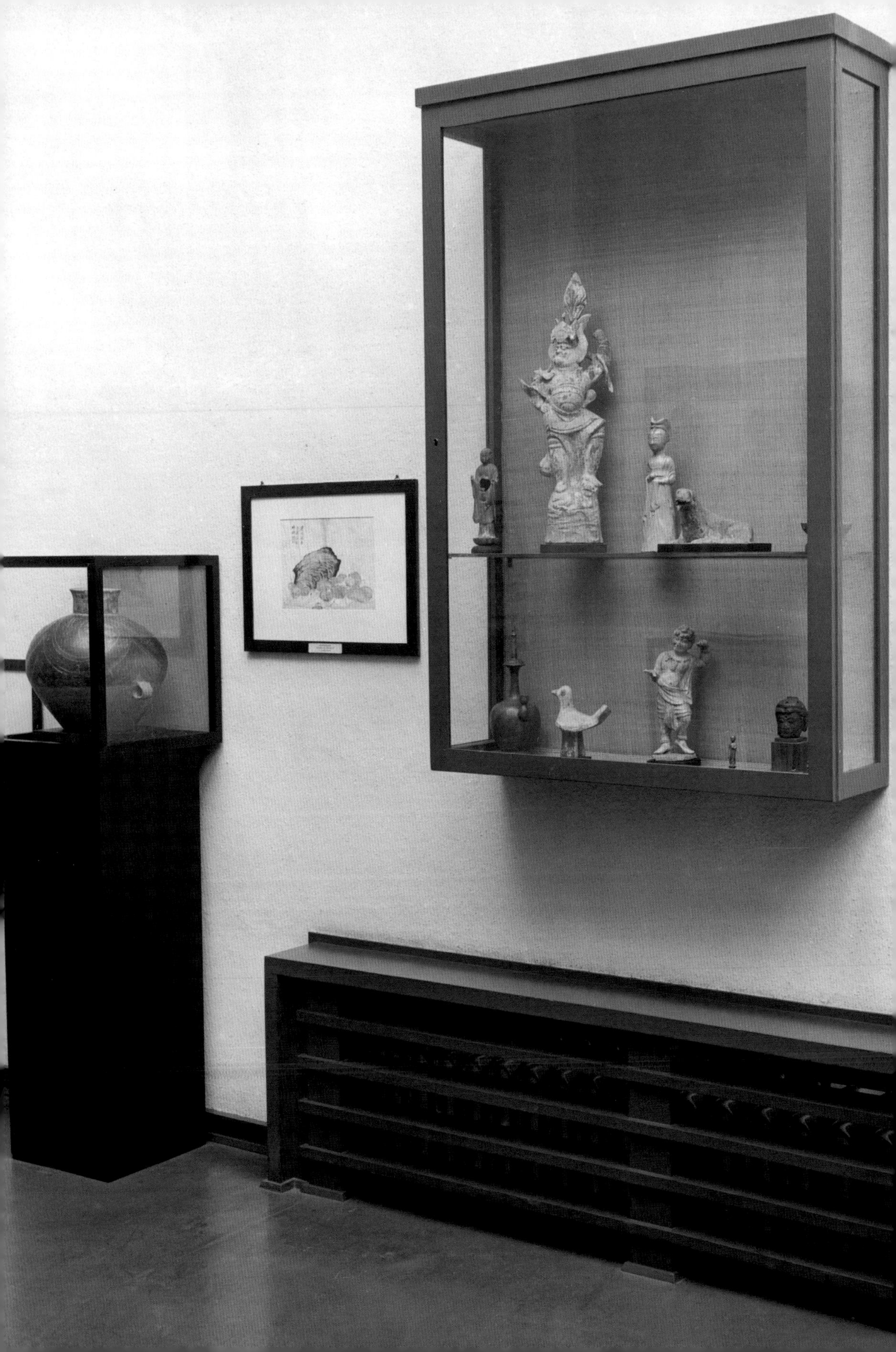

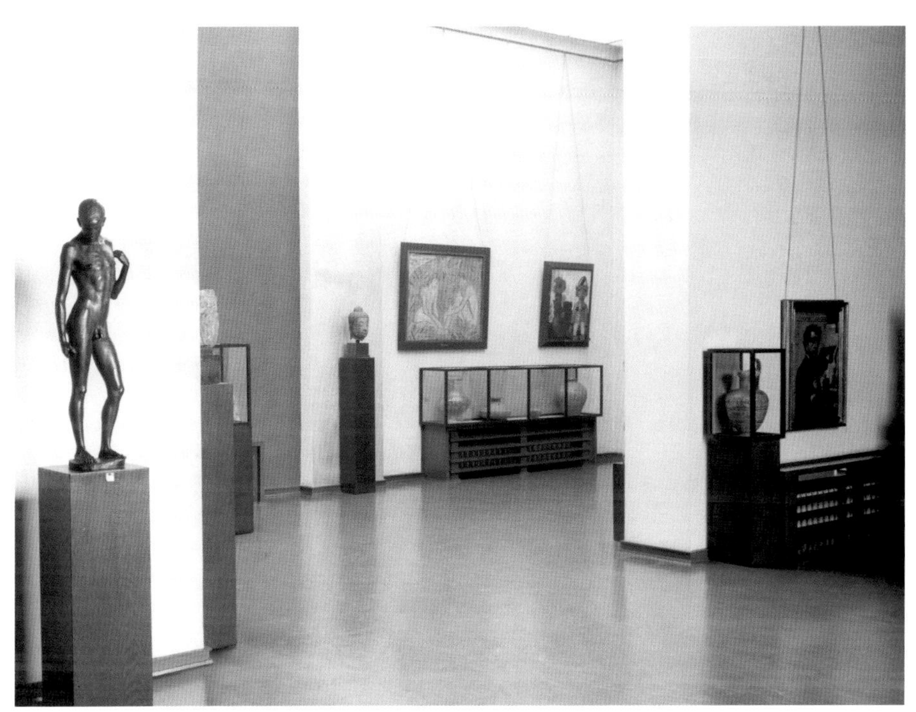

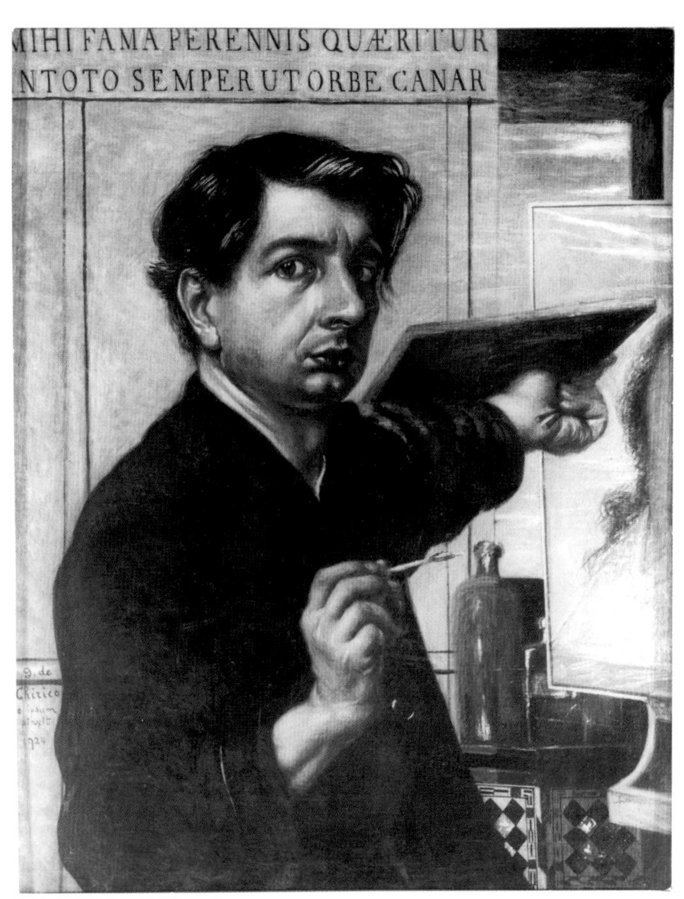
MIHI FAMA PERENNIS QUÆRITUR
N TOTO SEMPER UT ORBE CANAR

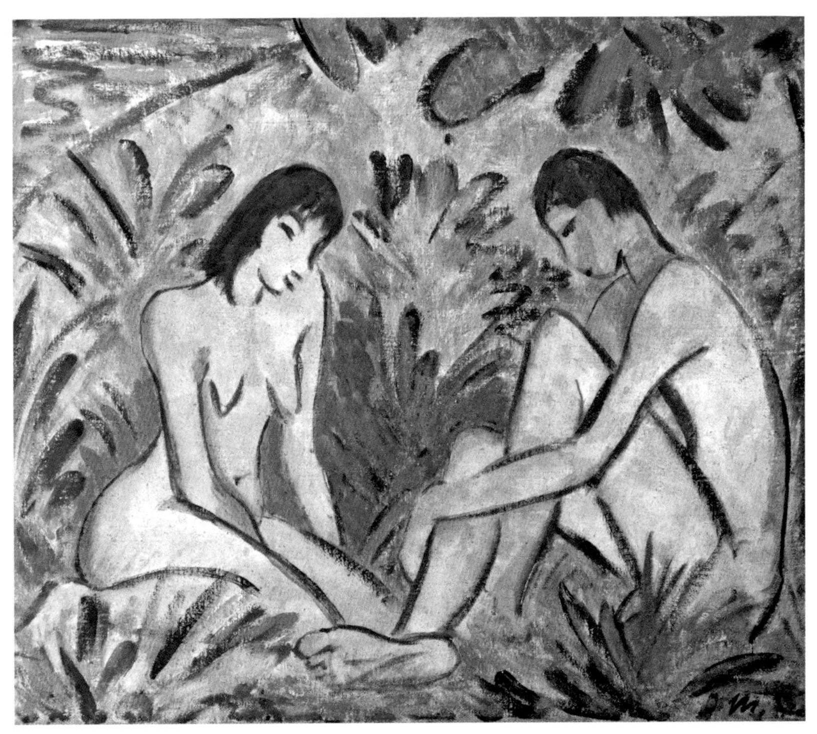

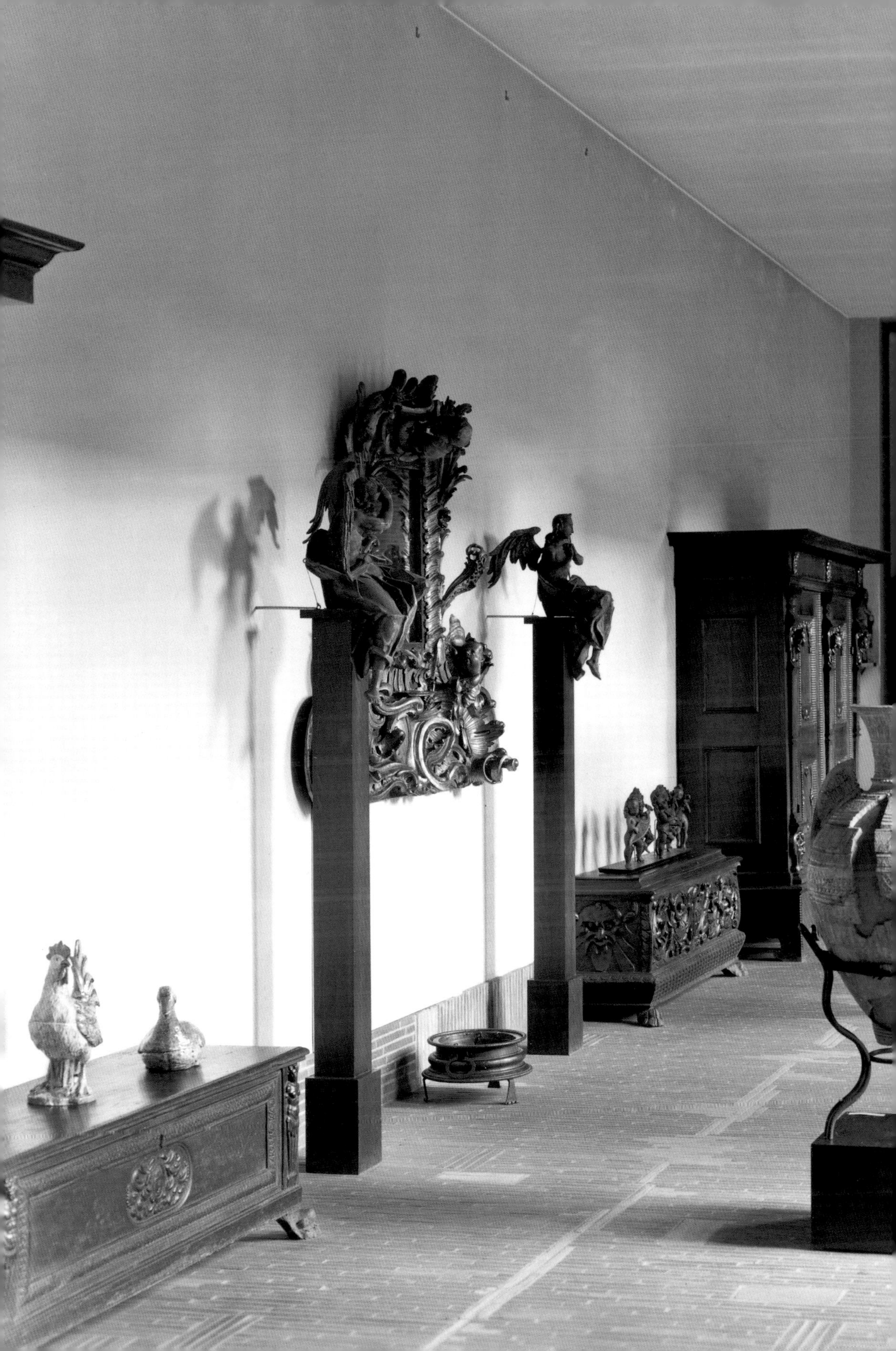

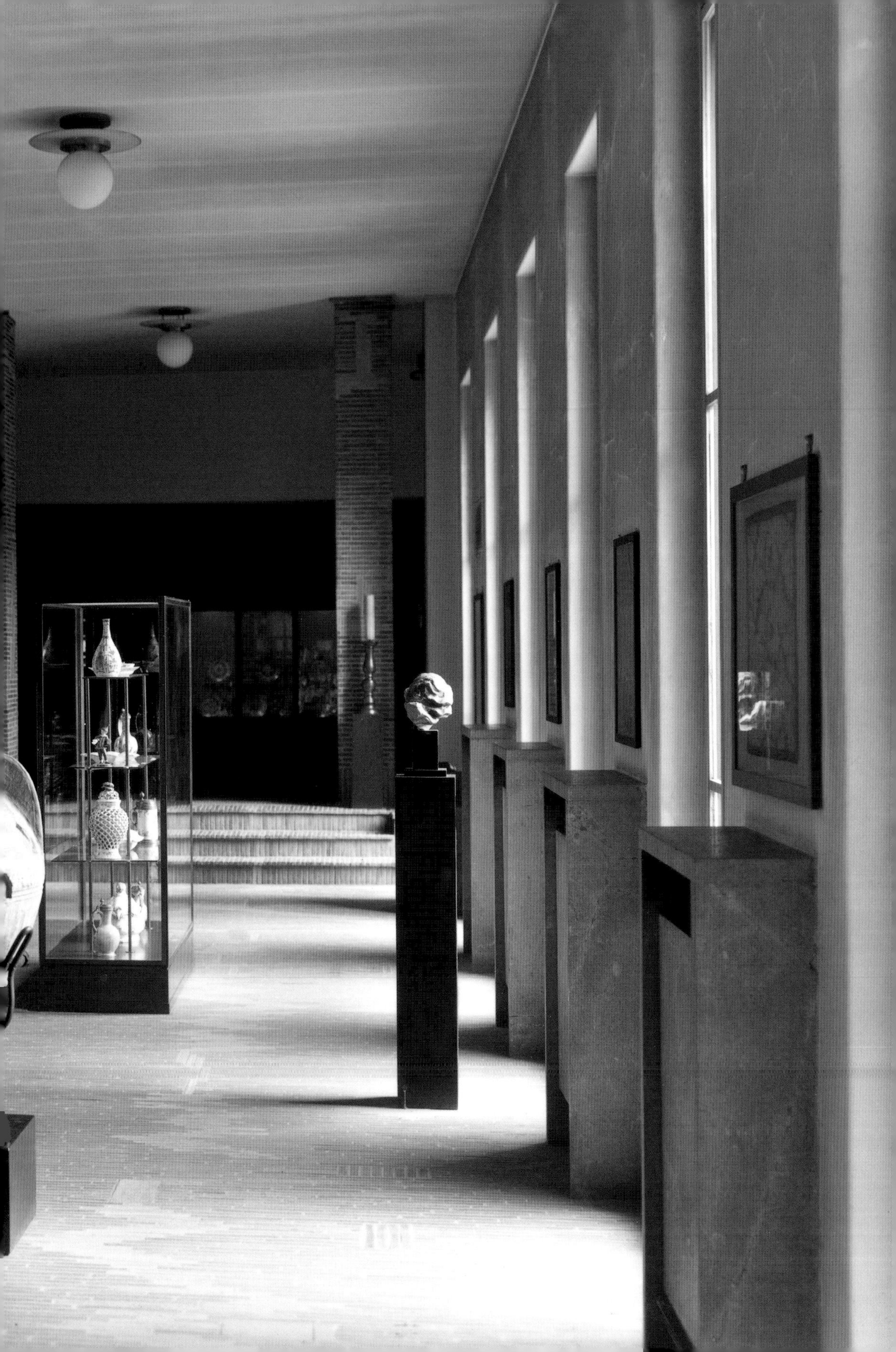

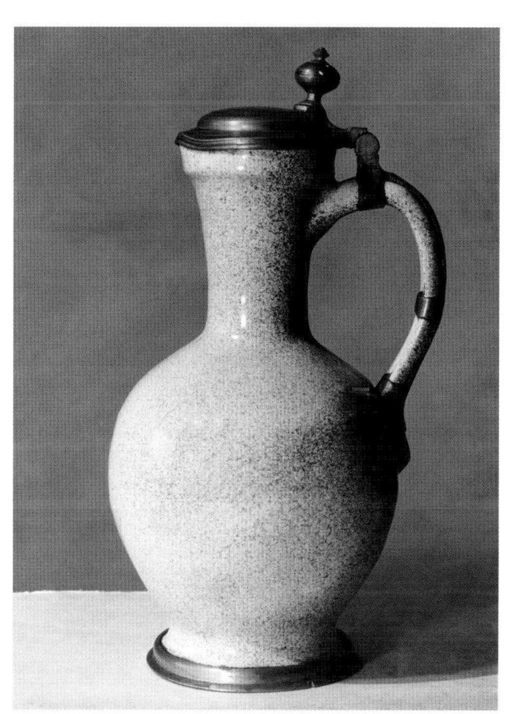

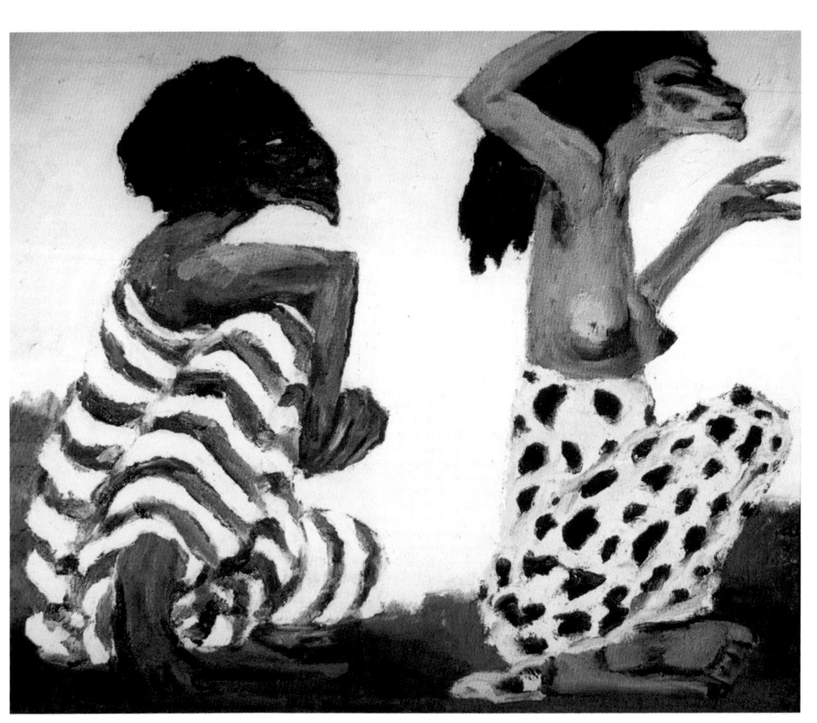

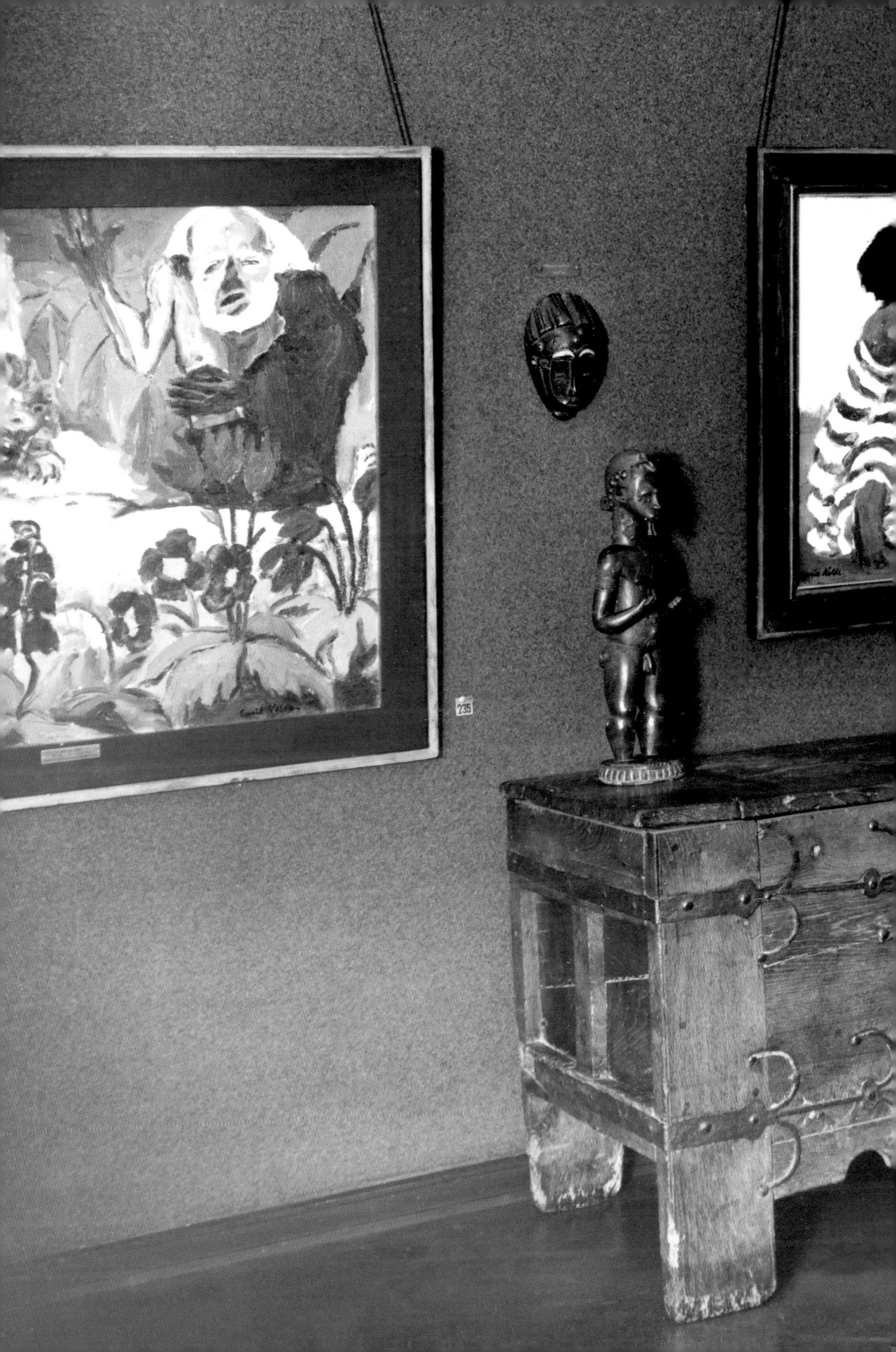

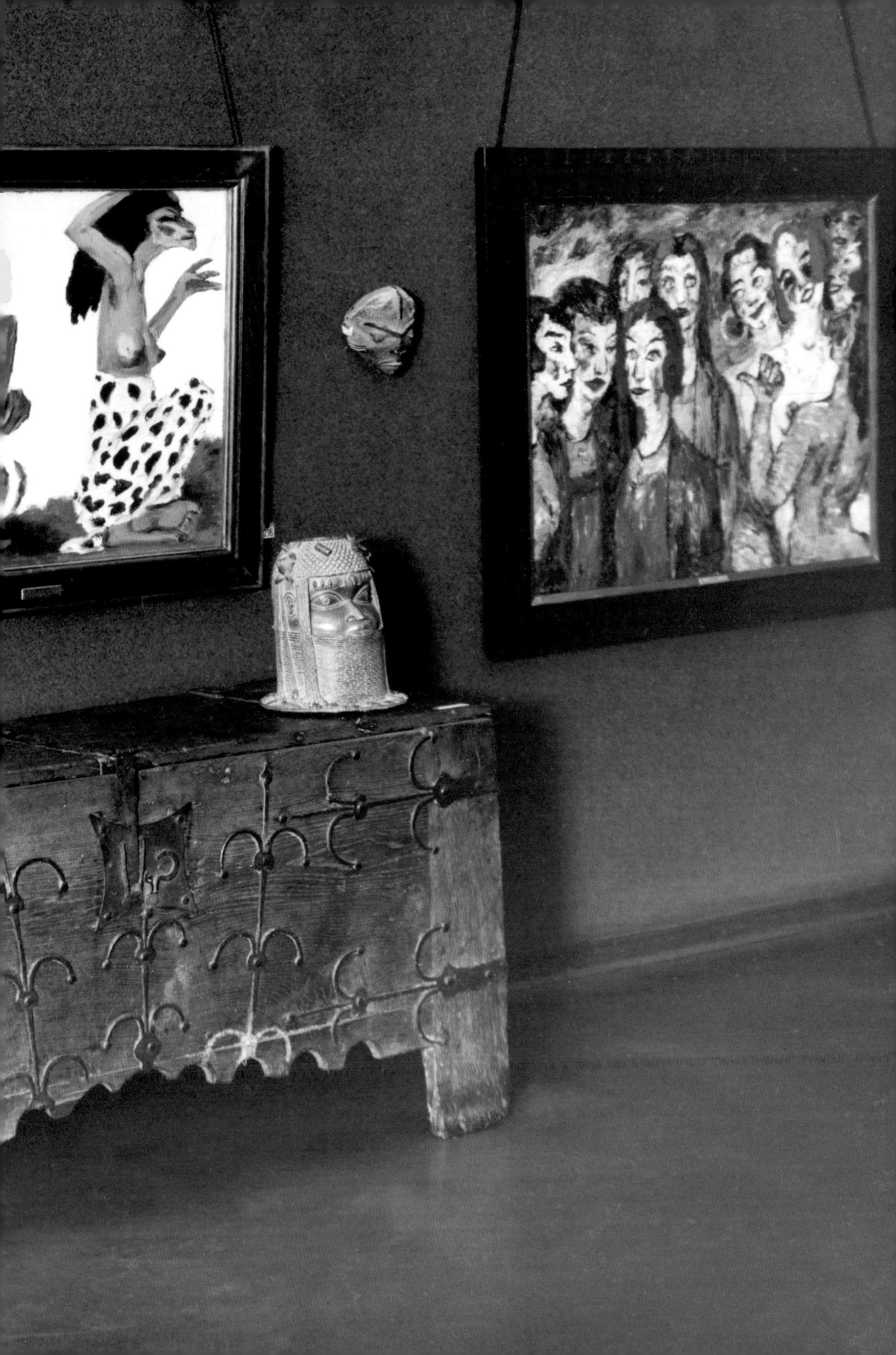

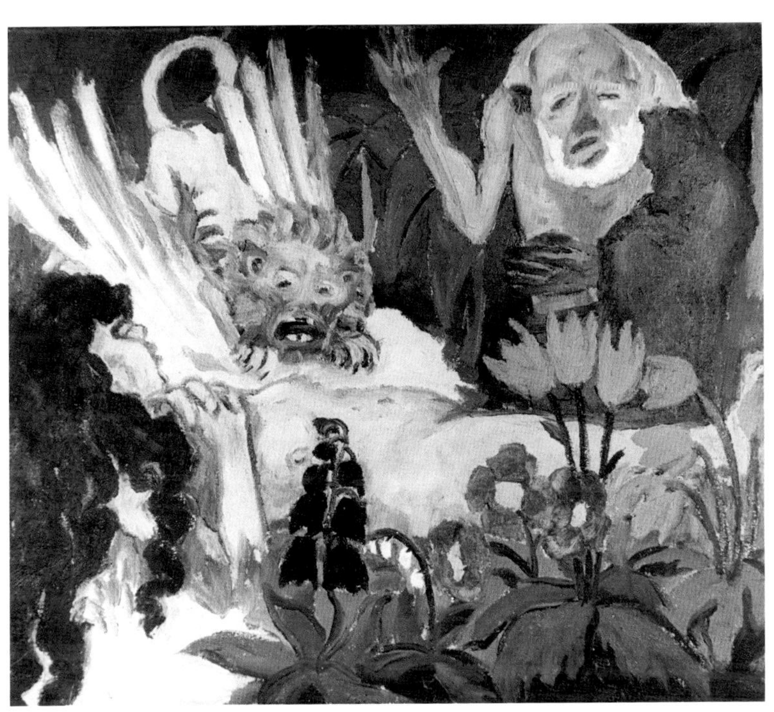

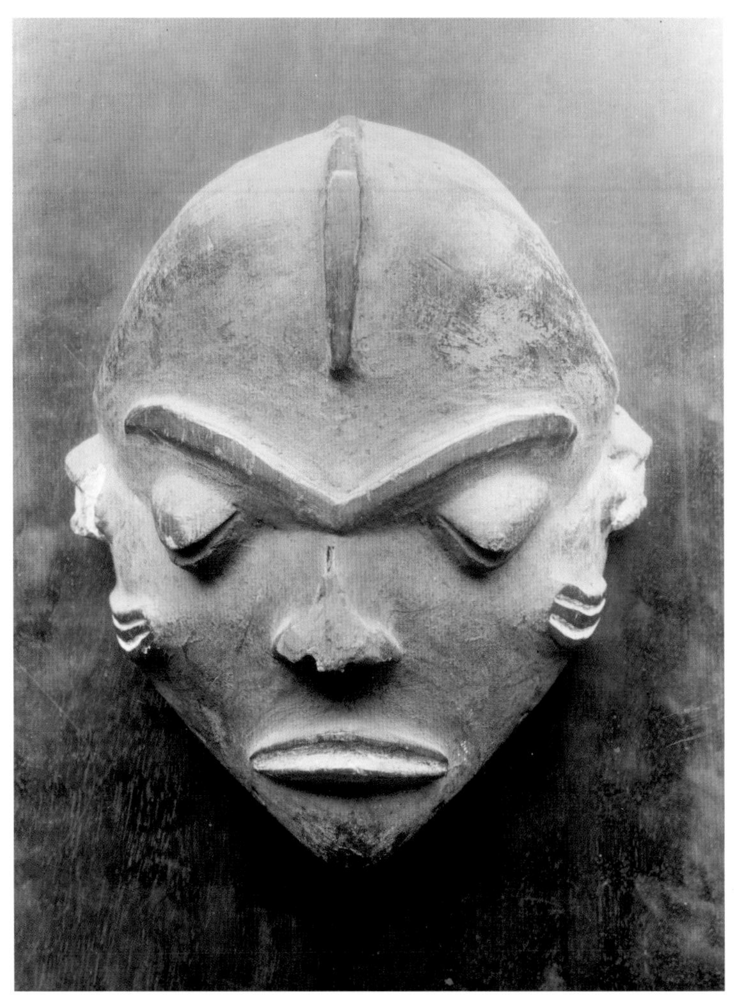

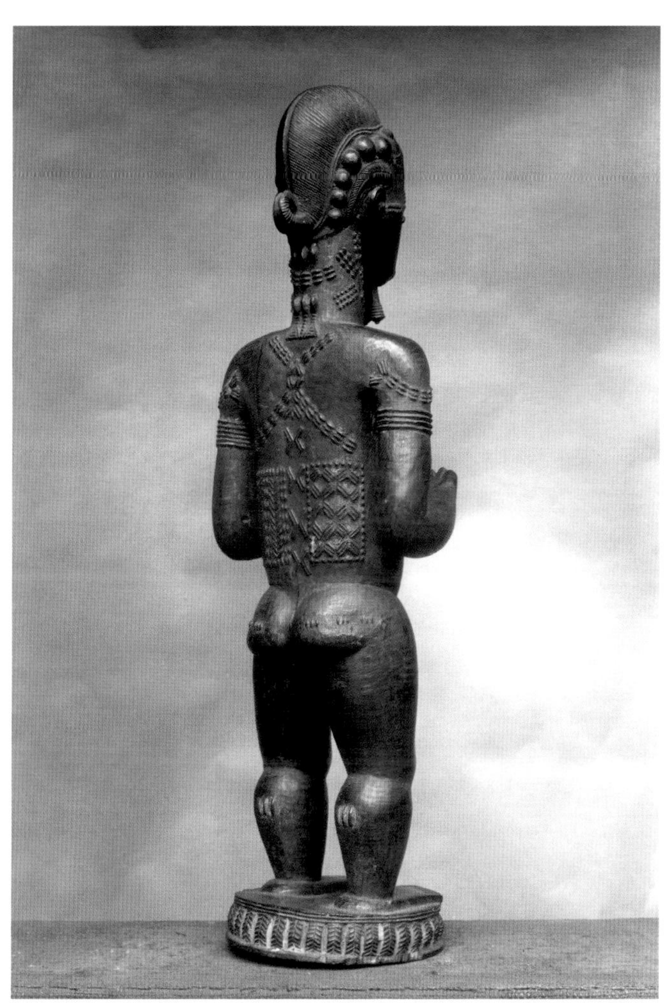

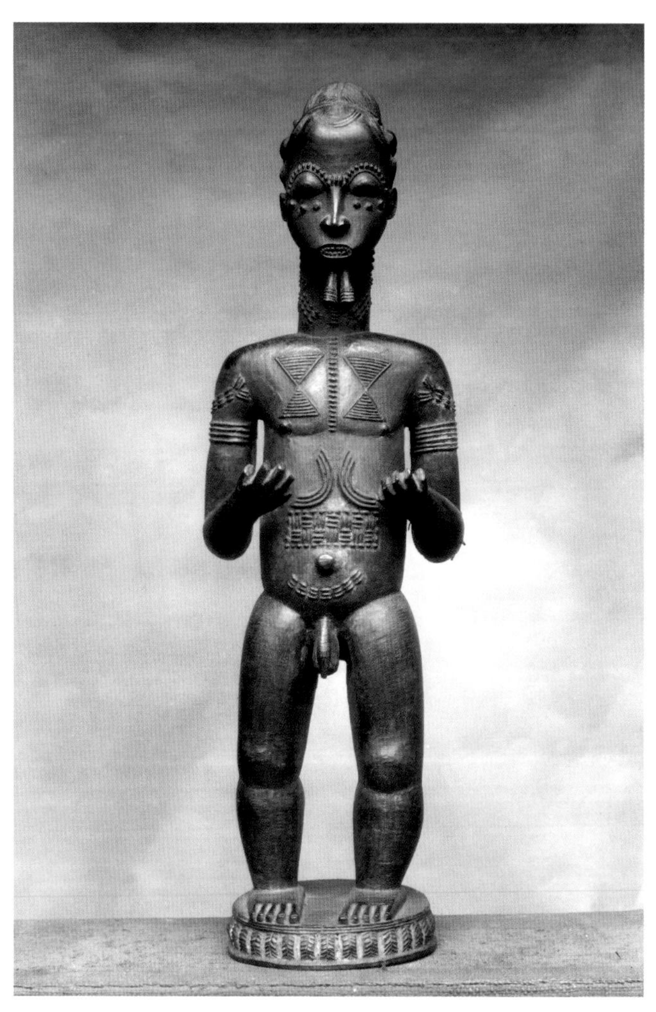

Vom Museum als Institution und Ort

Bruno Haas

Das Schicksal gab uns, schreibt Hegel, »mit den Werken der Kunst nicht ihre Welt mehr (...), sondern allein die eingehüllte Erinnerung dieser Wirklichkeit. – Unser Thun in ihrem Genusse ist daher (...) nur das äußerliche Thun, das von diesen Früchten etwa Regentropfen oder Stäubchen abwischt, und an die Stelle der inneren Elemente der umgebenden, erzeugenden und begeistenden Wirklichkeit das weitläufige Gerüste der todten Elemente der äusserlichen Existenz, der Sprache, des Geschichtlichen u. s. f. errichtet, nicht um sich in sie hinein zu leben, sondern nur, um sie in sich vorzustellen.«[1] Der Ort eines Kunstwerkes, das seine Welt verloren hat, ist das Museum. Der Weltverlust des Kunstwerks zeigt sich, an der Vitrine. Diese trennt den »Betrachter« vom Werk, es auf Dauer zu schützen, sie ist aber eigentlich die Spur eines Bruches; desjenigen Bruches, der unsere Welt von derjenigen trennt, in welcher das Werk entstand. In jene Welt kann nunmehr der Besucher nur noch sich »hineinversetzen«, indem er sich imaginär in die Nähe z. B. jenes Bodhisattva begibt (Abb. S. 24/25 und 28), d. h. in den Raum hinein, den die Vitrine anzeigt, welcher der eigene des Werkes wäre. Das Museum ist spätestens seit Hegels Zeiten durch diesen Bruch definiert: Es ist das Haus, worin solche Gegenstände aufbewahrt sind, die ihre Welt verloren haben, und zwar, insofern sie sie verloren haben. Es gibt aber, ebenfalls seit Hegels Tagen und vermutlich noch länger schon, eine Kunst, die ihrerseits geradezu und ausdrücklich für dieses Haus geschaffen ist. Diese Situation ist befremdlich. Sie wurde überhaupt erst ermöglicht durch jenen Weltverlust und wiederum dadurch, dass eine Kunst trotz ihres Weltverlustes und in ihrem Weltverlust für uns immer noch etwas ist, ja dass dieser Weltverlust selbst positiv zu unserer Welt dazugehört. Erst unter der Voraussetzung dieser Situation kann das Verhältnis von »Kunst und Leben« überhaupt zum Thema eines Nachdenkens werden. Bei der Frage, ob Kunst und Leben einander fremd oder nah, ob »Kunst und Leben« nach ihrer angeblichen Trennung wieder zur Einheit gebracht werden sollten, geht es um das Museum als Ort von Gegenständen, die ihre Welt verloren haben, und

von solchen, die für einen Ort geschaffen sind, an dem Gegenstände,
die ihre Welt verloren haben, aufbewahrt werden.

Was ist das Museum? Und warum werden Kunstwerke auch dann aufbewahrt, wenn sie ihre Welt verloren haben? Hegel vergleicht in dem
oben zitierten Text das Schicksal der nun weltlosen Kunst mit einem
Mädchen, das diese Kunst gleich Früchten darreicht. Und »wie das
Mädchen, das die gepflückten Früchte darreicht, mehr ist, als die in ihre
Bedingungen und Elemente ausgebreitete Natur derselben, welche sie
unmittelbar darbot, indem es diß alles in den Strahl des selbstbewußten
Auges und der darreichenden Gebehrde zusammenfaßt, so ist der Geist
des Schicksals, der uns jene Kunst darbietet, mehr als das sittliche
Leben und Wirklichkeit jenes Volkes...«, gemeint ist das griechische
Volk.[2] Demnach liegt also in dem entwurzelten Kunstwerk darin, daß es
entwurzelt ist, ein Mehr; und das Kunstwerk kann überhaupt solches
sein, was als entwurzeltes noch und gerade als solches eine Bedeutung
hat. Die Möglichkeit des Weltverlustes, nämlich die Möglichkeit, im
Weltverlust dennoch zu sein, einer anderen Welt anzugehören, diese
Möglichkeit gehört zum Wesen des Kunstwerks; und eben so gehört zu
unserer Welt die Möglichkeit, Kunstwerke, die ihre Welt verloren, zu
empfangen, das Museum.

Das Museum ist der einheimische Ort dieser Heimatlosigkeit. Diese
Funktion bildet in der Struktur der Institution Museum das ungehobene,
ungedachte Moment, das das Museum seit seinem Bestehen trägt
sowohl, und beunruhigt. Wir werden, was das heißt, aus einem Werk zu
lernen suchen, das dem Museum Folkwang gehört, einst, auf Renger-
Patzschs Fotografie gut sichtbar, im Vorgängerbau hing, später als
entartete Kunst verkauft, durch Wiederankauf in die Sammlung zurückkehrte und jetzt an rekonstruierter Stelle präsentiert ist: aus dem Selbstbildnis von Paula Modersohn-Becker. Wir werden fragen, was dieses
Bild hier zu tun habe.

Schon Hegels Zeit kennt eine eigentliche Museums-Kunst, eine Kunst,
die von Anfang an für gar keinen anderen Ort geschaffen ist, als das Museum. Dies gilt so gut für die akademische wie die nicht-akademische,
eventuell »avantgardistische« Kunst des 19. und 20. Jahrhunderts. Man

denke an einen Salonkünstler wie Ary Scheffer, der die letzten Jahre seines Lebens damit verbringt, eine Versuchung Christi zu malen, die zum vollkommenen Kunstwerk werden soll, oder an ein programmatisches Werk wie Gauguins *Woher kommen wir? ...*, das die Freunde des Meisters dem Musée du Luxembourg in Paris schenken wollten, weil es schlicht und einfach in keine Privatsammlung gehört.[3] Sobald aber Kunstwerke unmittelbar an das Museum adressiert werden, verändert sich dessen Funktion und korrelativ die Funktion und der Begriff der Kunst. Erst wo Kunstwerke, die ihre Welt verloren, für sich selbst hingestellt werden, kann die Kunst als ein absoluter Wert, d.h. als etwas, das nur an und für sich selbst gilt, als absolute Kunst überhaupt formuliert werden. Natürlich zeigt diese Absolutheit und Autonomie nur eine neue Art von Weltangehörigkeit an; die Kunst nimmt nunmehr als etwas Autonomes am »Leben« teil. Das l'art pour l'art wird später nur eine besondere Version dieser schon seit Anfang des 19. Jahrhunderts wohl etablierten und von Schelling und Hegel auch begrifflich erfassten Struktur sein.

Diese Form von Absolutheit definiert das Kunstwerk hiermit als einen *Wert*. Das bedeutet zunächst nichts anderes als dass das Kunstwerk eben »gilt«, dass es überhaupt als Kunstwerk gilt. Aber was heißt es, ein Kunstwerk zu sein? Dies bedeutet unter den nunmehr eintretenden Umständen nichts anderes, als ein *gültiges* Kunstwerk zu sein. Der Wert ist also nicht mehr nur eine Eigenschaft des Werks, sondern sein Wesen (definiens). Es ist kein Zufall, dass Diskussionen darüber, ob etwas überhaupt ein Kunstwerk sei, dadurch, dass es einen gewissen inneren Wert habe, überhaupt erst seit dem 19. Jahrhundert stattfinden. Natürlich streitet man auch früher schon darüber, wie richtig zu malen, zu schreiben, zu musizieren sei. Allein, es handelt sich dabei stets nur um die Ausführung von etwas, dessen Wesen als Gemälde, Musikstück oder Poesie gar nicht in Frage steht, also nicht um die Frage, ob etwas überhaupt »Kunst« sei; ja dieser abstrakte Begriff von »Kunst« steht erst seit dem 19. Jahrhundert zur Verfügung. Bei den Arbeiten eines Marcel Duchamp stellt sich die Frage: Ist das überhaupt Kunst? Es wird darauf geantwortet, indem man zeigt, sie seien gelungene, gültige Kunst, sie haben Wert.[4] Die »absolute« Kunst, die für das Museum geschaffen ist, wird insofern durch ihren Wert definiert. Das Neue ist nicht, dass Kunstwerke überhaupt einen Wert haben – schon die Alten

haben nach Plinius' Bericht für die Werke gewisser Meister sehr hohe Preise bezahlt –, sondern dass dieser Wert zum definiens der Kunst wird. Diese durchaus moderne Position begründet den spezifisch modernen Fetischcharakter des Kunstwerks. Die Institution dient dabei der Feststellung des Geltens künstlerischer Werte, in dem doppelten Sinne, dass sie auf Werte reagiert (öffentlich als kostbar, d. h. gültig bekannte Werke erwirbt und konserviert) oder Werte schafft (noch unbekannte Werke durch ihre Autorität konsakriert). Dabei versteht es sich von selbst, dass dieser Wert in einen ökonomischen muss übersetzt werden können. Der Fetischcharakter des modernen Kunstwerks ist also im Marx'schen Sinne des Fetischcharakters der Ware überhaupt zu verstehen, jedoch mit der Nuance, dass er im Falle des Kunstwerks zugleich als definiens desselben fungiert. – Der bloße »Wert« des Kunstwerks ist der leere das Kunstsein der Kunst konstituierende Signifikant, mag jener Wert im Übrigen begründet sein wie er will. Das Museum aber ist der Hort jenes abstrakten Wertes. Diese (neue) Funktion des Museums ersetzt die ältere Funktion als Ort der Kunst in ihrem Weltverlust nicht, sondern überwuchert sie nur.

Auf diese Funktion gründet sich der performative Charakter des Kunstwerks im spezifisch modernen und zeitgenössischen Sinne. Nach verschiedenen Definitionen, die allesamt dem weiteren Rahmen der konzeptuellen Kunst entstammen (z. B. bei Donald Judd, Joseph Kosuth, Sol LeWitt), ist etwas dadurch ein Kunstwerk, dass es dazu deklariert wird. Dabei ist der Term »Kunstwerk« an ihm selbst leer, aber das zum Kunstwerk deklarierte Objekt entfaltet, insofern es zum Kunstwerk deklariert ist, eine Arbeit des Sinnes, aus der sich entscheidet, ob es auch gültig, d. h. wirklich ein Kunstwerk sei. Das Werk reproduziert also (oder auch nicht) seinen Kunstcharakter, nämlich seinen abstrakten Wert durch solches, was selbst nicht abstrakter Wert ist. Der Term »Kunstwerk« funktioniert hier also als ein performativer. Die Institution ist aber nichts anderes als die Möglichkeit jenes perfomativen Aktes selbst. Kunsttheoretiker wie George Dickie, Arthur Coleman Danto, Jean-Marie Scheffer oder Yves Michaud haben deshalb in verschiedener Weise versucht, die Kunst als Funktion der Institution zu verstehen. Sie sind dabei Impulsen gefolgt, die wie gesehen aus der Kunst selbst hervorgegangen sind und die daher am besten in dieser Kunst analysiert werden.

Hieraus folgt eine eigenartige Stellung des Künstlers im Verhältnis zu seinem eigenen Werk. In gewisser Hinsicht müssen wir sagen, dass ein solches Werk gar keinen Autor hat, ganz in dem Sinne, in welchem Roland Barthes schon 1968 den »Tod« des Autors begrüßt.[5] Wir wollen betrachten, wie dieses Phänomen in der Arbeit von Simon Starling sich auswirkt. –

Wir sagten, das institutionell und performativ definierte Werk habe in gewisser Hinsicht gar keinen Autor. In gewisser Hinsicht, denn in einer anderen Hinsicht hat es ganz notwendig einen Autor: Es hat einen Autor, insofern es notwendig signiert sein, d. h. insofern jemand es zur Kunst erklären, die Verantwortung übernehmen muss. Dieser Umstand ist merkwürdig genug, zumal es bedeutende Kunstwerke gibt, die keinen identifizierbaren Autor haben und bei denen dieses Moment der Signatur und zu verantwortenden Urheberschaft offenbar keine Rolle spielt, man denke nur an die ägyptischen Pyramiden oder an manches Meisterwerke romanischer Baukunst. Im Rahmen des hier erläuterten performativen Kunstbegriffs ist die Signatur dagegen ein notwendiges Moment. Einerseits ist sie nur eine formale, inhaltsleere Bedingung des Kunstwerks, das, ist es einmal als solches gesetzt, nun durch sein wirkliches Funktionieren beweisen muss, dass es ein gutes, d. h. wertvolles Kunstwerk, also im Grunde überhaupt eines ist. Es ist insofern gleichgültig, wer das Werk signiert, wenn es nur irgend signiert ist. Andererseits soll das Kunstwerk wirklich gelten, d. h. eine Gemeinschaft von Rezipienten muss von seinem Wert überzeugt sein, sich dafür interessieren, daran glauben. Aber der Künstler selbst muss am meisten daran glauben und stellt dies durch ein persönliches Engagement unter Beweis. Nur durch solch ein Engagement hat die Signatur den notwendigen »Wert« und das gehörige »Gewicht«. Der Name des Künstlers wird hier also umgekehrt sehr persönlich genommen. Beide Aspekte der Signatur scheinen grundsätzlich in allen nur irgendwie auf den institutionellen Kunstbegriff bezogenen Kunstpraktiken ihren Ort zu haben.

Dennoch hat solche performative und institutionell definierte Kunst zugleich strukturell keinen Autor. Dies betrachten wir an Simon Starlings Arbeit. Es gibt hier einen historischen Zusammenhang, der einfach aufgearbeitet, d. h. eigentlich nur präsentiert wird: Der teilrekonstruierte

Vorgängerbau des Architekten Eduard Körner, der im Krieg zerstört worden ist, Kunstwerke, von denen einige an ihrem Platz fehlen, weil sie als entartete Kunst verkauft worden sind, also Spuren der Geschichte, sodann ein bedeutender Fotograf, Albert Renger-Patzsch, nach dessen Bildern die Rekonstruktion vorgenommen wurde, und dessen Blick auf die Werke im Rahmen einer Arbeit, der es um die Institution, das Rezipieren der Kunst u. dgl. m. geht, besonders interessant ist. Ferner ist da der besonders gelungene Neubau von 1960 und daneben der Ergänzungsbau von 1983 (in dem Starlings Arbeit installiert ist), der noch in diesem Jahr abgerissen wird, um durch einen Neubau ersetzt zu werden. Allein durch ihre Präsenz im Museum Folkwang stellt diese Arbeit die Frage nach der Zukunft des Museums und der Kunst. Alle diese Elemente sprechen für sich und werden zum Sprechen gebracht dadurch, dass sie versammelt sind. Dabei spielt es nur eine unwesentliche Rolle, wie weit der Künstler die versammelten Parameter überblickt oder beherrscht. Im Gegenteil, diese gehen strukturell über seinen Horizont hinaus, handelt es sich doch um historische Fakten. Damit verlässt der Autor die für Roland Barthes ohnehin nur imaginäre Position des identischen Autoren, der, was er sagt, auch verantworten kann, und um dessen persönliche Intention es zu tun sei. »Der Text ist eine Sammlung von Zitaten, hervorgegangen aus den tausend Foren der Kultur. Wie Bouvard und Pécuchet, diese ewigen Kopisten, erhaben und komisch zugleich, aber ihre Lächerlichkeit zeigt präzise die Wahrheit des Schreibens an –, so kann jeder Autor stets nur einen ihm vorausgehenden Gestus imitieren«,[6] und etwas vorher: »Was da spricht, das ist die Sprache, nicht der Autor«.[7] Die Einheit des Textes konstituiert sich damit nach Barthes nicht länger im Autor, sondern im Leser, insofern dieser den Text entwirrt und artikuliert, d. h. letztlich strukturalistisch analysiert (also die verschiedenen, darin zusammengeführten Quellen sondert und aufeinander bezieht). Der Autor (auctor) verliert seine Autorität (auctoritas). Auch Simon Starling macht sich nicht zu einem Autor im traditionellen Sinn, sondern fungiert eigentlich als Leser, als die Mitte eines Zusammentreffens verschiedener Reden, die er nur versammelt, deren jede aber für sich selbst spricht. Und gleichwohl spricht Starling in diesem Konzert auch für sich, d. h. übernimmt als Autor eine Verantwortung, und zwar durch seine bloße Signatur präzise die Verantwortung des Ganzen als eines Kunstwerkes.

Seine Beteiligung am Ganzen wird, insofern er seiner auctoritas verlustig ging, zu einem signifikanten *Moment* desselben. Grammatisch tritt er uns hierdurch wesentlich in der dritten Person entgegen, als derjenige, an dessen Tun und Lassen sich etwas zeigt. Dieses Tun und Lassen ist das wirkliche Tun und Lassen des Individuums Simon Starling, das hierbei in gewissen Grenzen eine »Geschichte« erzeugt, die man etwa durch Interviews mehr oder weniger in Erfahrung bringen kann, die sich aber signifikant genug auch in den Dokumenten seiner Arbeit niederlegt. Hier hat der Künstlerdiskurs als eigenständige zeitgenössische Textgattung seinen Ort. Bei Simon Starling ist diese »Geschichte« durch ein besonders luzides Verhältnis zur Problematik des Autoren ausgezeichnet. In der Tat tritt dieser bei Starling in den meisten, wenn nicht in allen seinen Arbeiten, gedoppelt auf.

Der Autor verdoppelt sich: Er trifft auf einen anderen Autor, welcher diese Rolle noch in einem traditionellen Sinne gespielt hat: z. B. auf Renger-Patzsch. Man vergleiche aber Starlings Repliken nach Designobjekten (Josef Frank, Poul Henningsen), oder kompliziertere Arbeiten, wo z. B. der Kühler des von Carlo Mollino für das Rennen in Le Mans von 1955 entworfenen Bisiluro rekonstruiert und, auf einen roten Fiat Panda von 1986 montiert, 24 Stunden lang über die Tangente von Turin gefahren wird,[8] oder wo »Mr Jeanneret« (Le Corbusier) Mr Naujok trifft: d. h. einfach das zur Zeit leerstehende Atelier von Le Corbusier an der Ste Baume (Provence) der bescheidenen Bauernstelle von Mr Naujok gegenüberliegt.[9] Bei dieser Publikation werden die historischen Elemente, die in der Installation zusammengeführt sind, und in dessen Zentrum eigentlich das von Mikaël Pedersen 1897 konstruierte Fahrrad steht, sogar im Wortsinn durch eine *Erzählung* verknüpft, d. h. durch einen Text, der ein Treffen jener beiden Herren fingiert und erzählt. Dieser Text ist dazu noch mit Annotationen versehen, welche historische Hintergrundinformationen geben. Die Anmerkungen sind nicht vom Künstler verfasst, d. h. fallen hierdurch in dem oben spezifizierten Sinne nicht mehr unter seine auctoritas. Dabei sind Text und begleitende Fotografien mit solcher Aufmerksamkeit behandelt, dass sie durchaus für sich stehen könnten. – In dem Gespann des Autors und seines Doppels haben die beiden Seiten einen ungleichen Wert. Der Andere Autor (der in den meisten Fällen schon verstorben ist: Le Corbusier, Carlo

Mollino, Charles Eames, dagegen jedoch auch einmal der ältere Zeitgenosse Chris Burden) hat ein besonderes Prestige, eben diejenige Autorität, die eine traditionelle Autorschaft begründen kann. Der Eine Autor aber (der Künstler, Simon Starling) behandelt jenen gerade als das, was er ist, als Phantom. Das Phantom des Anderen Autors gründet die sonach geliehene (uneigentliche) Autorschaft des Einen Autors. Diese aber inauguriert ganz alleine das Ereignis und Gelten (den »Wert«) des Ganzen als eines Kunstwerks.

Der Autor, so möchten wir sagen, entflieht, verwandelt sich in eine dritte Person, spricht nicht mehr geradewegs mit seinem Publikum; er verwandelt sich in ein Symptom, wenn anders das Symptom das ist, woran sich etwas anderes zeigt, das mit diesem »zusammen«, ab»fällt«.[10]

Was hier faktisch in der Praxis eines zeitgenössischen Künstlers geschieht, hat einen theoriegeschichtlichen Hintergrund. In der Tat bereitet die institutionelle Kunsttheorie den Boden für diese neue Situation der Kunstrezeption, die selbstverständlich nicht nur den Autor, sondern auch das Publikum und seine rezipierende Haltung und Erwartung betrifft. Der Abbau des älteren Autonomieanspruches ist das Korrelat der veränderten Fragestellung. Insofern man fragt, wie eine Gemeinschaft sich auf den Kunstgegenstand bezieht, indem man also diese Beziehung objektiviert, stellt man eine neue Art von Beziehung zum Artefakt her, und zwar eine indirekte. In dieser indirekten Perspektive erscheint das Werk natürlich anders als in der direkten des »naiven« Rezipienten. Während dieser vom Werk gefesselt wird, bleibt der institutionelle Kunsttheoretiker »frei«, d. h. entzieht sich dem von ihm durch seine Fragestellung eingeklammerten unmittelbaren Anspruch des Kunstobjektes. Er entzieht sich diesem Anspruch strukturell durch seine Frage; denn sobald man den Anspruch nicht auf sich selbst, sondern nur auf eine dritte Person bezieht, auf den »Rezipienten«, den »Autor«, die »Institution« usw., die hier auch grammatisch immer in der dritten Person auftreten, handelt es sich nicht mehr um einen Anspruch, der uns selbst anspricht. Die institutionskritische Relativierung des absoluten Anspruches der Kunst ist in diesem Sinne also nicht das Ergebnis ihrer Arbeit, sondern die Voraussetzung.[11] Sie inauguriert damit eine neue Situation der Kunst, d. h. weit davon entfernt, nur eine »objektive« Be-

schreibung der Strukturen zu sein, die in der Kunst ohnehin wirksam sind, wirkt sie selbst als Performativ. Die Situation, die sie inauguriert, geht wie jede andere das Subjekt auch direkt an; nur ist, was es direkt angeht, jetzt affirmativ durch den performativen, institutionellen Kunstbegriff definiert, mit Folgen für die Position des Autors, die wir anhand von Starlings Arbeit oben zu beschreiben versucht haben.

Auch Simon Starlings Arbeit ist als eine institutionstheoretische beschreibbar, die der Theorie selbst mindestens dies voraus hat, dass sie ihren eigenen performativen Beitrag nicht verdrängt, sondern gerade offenlegt, geschehen lässt. Man beachte, wie die Kunstwerke des Museum Folkwang in seiner Arbeit auftreten, nämlich als Gegenstände einer intentio obliqua, einer indirekten Wahrnehmung. Wir sehen, wie z. B. Renger-Patzsch diese Werke gesehen hat, aber nicht unmittelbar diese Werke selbst. Selbstverständlich sieht man sie, indem man sie so sieht wie Renger-Patzsch sie gesehen hat, ganz und gar nicht so, wie er sie gesehen hat, denn er sah die Werke im Gegensatz zu uns geradewegs. –

Und was geschieht? Es kommt zu einem Ereignis.[12] Von diesem Ereignis wollen wir nur sagen, dass es uns inmitten der Geschichte und Geschichten einfach dasein lässt. Alle Umstände nehmen teil an diesem Ereignis: der ausstehende Abriss des Ergänzungsbaus von 1983, die Zukunft des Neubaus, die Vergangenheit des Altbaus, die bewegte Geschichte der Sammlung, der Blick des Fotografen. Das Ereignis der Ausstellung ist nur ein flüchtiger Moment, nichts endgültiges. Das Ereignis hat eine Zeit. Welche Zeit? Eine andere Zeit als die alltägliche, eine Zeit, die aus der alltäglichen Zeit herausgehalten ist. Die herausgehaltene Zeit dieses Ereignisses vergeht nicht. Sie ist eigentlich *Zahl*. Was ist eine Zahl? Zahlen spielen im ganzen Werk von Simon Starling eine große Rolle. Überall wird datiert, der Körner-Bau so gut wie der Bisiluro in der oben zitierten Turiner Arbeit, und diese so gut wie Pedersons Fahrrad. Die Zahl hat mit der Sache nichts zu tun, noch weniger als der Name. Zahlen sind relativ. Aber gerade dadurch sagen uns die Zahlen, wo wir hingehören. Wir sind aber das, wo wir hingehören, wenn anders das menschliche Sein ein Da-sein ist. Weil das Jahr 2007 eine Zahl hat, kann es auch künftig dasselbe Jahr bleiben, das es ist.

53

Könnte man die Zeit nicht zählen, sie würde nicht vergehen und deswe-
gen noch weniger aufgehoben dieselbe bleiben können. Die Zeit wird
er-*zählt*. Die er-zählte Zeit wird eigens hergestellt durch ein Kunstwerk,
das sie sich ereignen lässt. Sie ist »Kunst«. –

Wir haben die Stratifikation der verschiedenen Funktionen des Kunst-
museums auseinandergelegt, um ein gewisses, sehr unauffälliges Ereignis zu bezeichnen, das sich im Ereignis dieser Ausstellung mitereignet.
Ich weiß nicht, ob dieses Ereignis von Simon Starling »gemeint« ist,
aber das spielt gar keine Rolle, insofern er ohnehin auf die Position
eines »meinenden« Autoren verzichtet. Der Autor dieses Textes ver-
meint und hofft, indem er dieses Nebenereignis eigens nennt und her-
vorhebt, mit dem Werk des Künstlers in ein Gespräch zu treten, d. h. auf
einen Anspruch desselben zu hören, und wiederum mit einer Frage auf
es zurückzukommen.

Das Ereignis besteht schlicht darin, dass in dieser Installation das
Selbstportrait von Paula Modersohn-Becker nicht an seinem Ort hängt.

Das Selbstbildnis von Paula Modersohn-Becker ist ein bedeutendes
Kunstwerk. Wir wollen sehen, in welcher Weise es in das Museum gehört, d. h. in welcher Weise es da ist, wo es ist. Um dies zu erfahren,
wenden wir uns an dieses Bild selbst.

Es handelt sich um ein Selbstbildnis. Das Gesicht auf dem Bild scheint
uns anzublicken. Der Blick stellt eine Anfrage, auf die wir eingehen können oder auch nicht. Wenn wir darauf eingehen, treten wir in den Ge-
sichtskreis der auf dem Bild dargestellten Person. Dann kommen wir
in eine gewisse Nähe zu dem Kunstwerk. Wie ist diese Nähe beschaf-
fen? – Sobald ich in den Kreis dieser Nähe trete, drängt sich mir das
Gefühl auf: umfasst zu sein vom dem Bild. D.h., es gibt nicht nur vor
mir etwas zu sehen, sondern auch hinter mir, etwas, das ich freilich nicht
sehen kann, solange es hinter mir bleibt. Was mich umfasst, ist ein
warmes, etwas abgetöntes Olivgrün. Dieses Olivgrün spiegelt sich auf

dem Gesicht der dargestellten Person, im Schatten, auf den Nasenflügeln, auf der Stirn. Es ist dort teils mit einem Orange vermischt. Zu diesem Grün gehört ein Licht, ein warmes, etwas schweres Innenlicht, wir sind in einem Zimmer. Dieses innere Licht ist von ganz anderer Natur als das helle blaue Licht, das von hinter der Person hereinfällt: das Tageslicht. Ein heller Vorhang verdeckt das Fenster in dem Zimmer; das Gesicht steht im Gegenlicht, wird selbst von dem schwächeren Grünschimmer getroffen, der von hinter mir selbst herkommt. Hinter mir ist Grün.

Aber es gibt auch ein Licht, das von unten heraufkommt, das Gesicht von unten erhellt. Dieses Licht ist heller als das matte schattige Grün, es hat einen gelblich-rötlichen Charakter. Es ist zwischen mir und der Person im Bild. Das Bild empfängt diese drei Lichter, nimmt sie auf, hält sie in sich. Es ist fest gebaut, gezeichnet. Die Zeichnung ist schwarz. An manchen Stellen wechselt das Schwarz mit Braun ab, z. B. am Haar, das gibt ihr eine gewisse skulpturale Massivität. Auf dieses Schwarz-Braun bezieht sich außerdem das Weiß, das in allerhand Vermischungen, aber kaum rein vorkommt. Ein geheimer Ort, auf den wir zurückkommen werden, bildet den Mittelpunkt dieser zeichnerischen Armatur: das Grau im linken Auge. Wir sagen, dies ist das zeichnerische Gerüste, die Armatur, in welche die drei Lichter eingetragen sind. Diese drei Lichter stellen mich an einen bestimmten Ort, nehmen mich in das Bild hinein. Sie tun dies in einer geheimnisvollen Weise, die keineswegs schon angemessen beschrieben ist. Das Grün, das mich umfasst, ist nicht bloß die Farbe eines Reflexes auf dem Gesicht, der logischerweise von hinter mir kommen muss. Diese Farbe hat auch einen eigentümlichen Bezug zu dem Ockerbeige des Malgrundes. Nimmt man noch das Preußischblau hinzu, wo es zum Schwarzen tendiert, so zeigt sich: diese drei Farben bilden eine Familie; sie erwecken eine Grundatmosphäre in dem Bild, in welche das Tageslicht durch den blauen Vorhang als ein Anderes, als ein Hinzukommendes hineinfällt. Insofern das Grün hinter mir ist, das Ockerbeige des Malgrundes ihm antwortet, insofern hebt es mich in die Intimität dieses Bildes. Ich gehe in die Dauer seiner Zeit ein. Dasjenige, was diese Dauer gibt, in die ich als in die Nähe des Bildes eingehe, nenne ich die *Bedauer*. In seinem Bezug zum Ockerbeige des Malgrundes und zum dunklen Preußischblau ist das Grün die Bedauer. Inmitten der Nähe des Bildes ist ein Feuer. Das dritte Licht, das von

unten jenes Gesicht erhellt, gelblich und eigentlich rot, es brennt da,
wo das Bild längst abbricht, eingerahmt von den zwei schwarzen Strei-
fen, die vage genug das Kleid der Person darstellen. Hier, nämlich ganz
unten links, stehen die Initialen »P M B«. Dieses in Schwarz eingerahmte
rote Feuer ist eigentlich das Schwergewicht des Bildes. Aus diesem
Brand steigt empor der Zweig der Kamelie: zwei Blätter berühren sich,
rechts; drei Blätter hängen nebeneinander, links; ein Blatt steht in der
Mitte, oben. An diesem Zweig beginnt man zu zählen. Was ist das, eine
Zahl? Warum entsteigt die Zahl dem Brand, getragen von einer Hand,
kaum skizziert, die das Verletzlichste ist und das Zarteste auf diesem
Bild. Das Eigene der Zahl ist, dass sie situiert, ohne doch den gerings-
ten Wesensbezug zur situierten Sache zu haben. Ich kann z. B. der
zweite Sohn meiner Eltern sein und dadurch aller Privilegien der Erstge-
burt verlustig gehen; aber nichts an meiner Natur macht mich zum zwei-
ten. Die Zahl hat nichts mit uns zu tun; aber sie situiert uns; sie wird
dadurch zum Schicksal. Der Zweig in der Hand von Paula Modersohn-
Becker stellt ein paar Zahlen zwischen uns: zwei, drei; das letzte Blatt
aber ist schwer zu zählen: d. h. schwer in der Zahl zu situieren. Er hält
die Mitte zwischen zwei Seiten und müsste demnach von ungerader,
»männlicher« Zahl sein wie die alten Arithmetiker sagten; es sind aber,
alle zusammen, genau sechs.

Die beiden Augen der Paula Modersohn-Becker haben einen verschiedenen Ausdruck. Ihr rechtes Auge ist müde und resigniert, gleich als
sähe es nichts mehr, das linke dagegen ist wach und sehend. Eben so
die Ohren. Das rechte Ohr, uns entgegengekehrt, ist wie eine leere, rötlich anlaufende wunde Stelle, taub: Das linke aber, kaum zu sehen, weil
abgewandt, hörend. Natürlich gehören beide Augen und beide Ohren
zu derselben Person, unsere Beschreibung ist übertrieben. Dennoch,
es gibt in dieser Person eine Zweiheit, eine Teilung. Diese wird durch
einen unauffälligen Strich im Vorhang, rechts oberhalb des Scheitels
merkwürdig unterstrichen.

Das rechte Auge, sagten wir, ist wie blind. Diese Blindheit, so fügen wir
jetzt hinzu, wird treffend durch den tonlosen Klang des neutralen Arti-
kels ausgedrückt, »das«. Das andere Auge ist sehend, oder wie man
auch sagt, es leuchtet. Dieses Leuchten wollen wir durch den femininen

Artikel sagen, »die«: die Auge. *Die* Auge ist von einem Grau, das sonst nirgends im Bild vorkommt. *Das* Auge ist auch grau, aber etwas bräunlicher. Eigentlich ist die Farbe Grau »farblos« wie man sagt. Dieses Grau aber ist in einer seltsamen, unsäglichen Weise leuchtend. Dieses unsägliche Leuchten des Grau wollen wir sagen, wenn wir sagen »die Auge«. Αὐγή (femininum) heißt auf Griechisch der Glanz, z. B. der überwältigende Glanz der Sonne.

Was aber liegt im Strahl des selbstbewussten Auges, in der darreichenden Gebärde? –

Der Mund ist rot. Was würde diese Person sprechen, wenn sie ihren Mund öffnete? Wir wissen es nicht. Weiß sie es selbst? Ist dies eine Person, die weiß, was sie will? Vielleicht nicht. Vielleicht nicht in dem Sinne, dass ihr *Wille* immer mit sich selbst und mit den Umständen übereinstimmt. Was dieser Mund sprechen wird, könnte sich etwa widersprechen. Es ist eine Schwebe darin. Stehen nicht auch das Auge und die Auge in einem Unterschied? Es gibt in dieser Person keinen Willen als wollte sie etwas Definiertes und demnach auch Widerspruchsfreies, Einheitliches, einen Gegenstand. Aber es gibt in ihr eine Entschiedenheit, jenseits des Willens, Entschiedenheit zu einem Weg. Diese Entschiedenheit schweigt und spricht aus der zart blauen Schwebe des Hintergrundes. Das Rot des Mundes steht vor dem Blau des Schleiers, der das Licht des Tages von dem »Brand« trennt. Diese Trennung öffnet den Raum, worin die Person da ist. Das, wo etwas sein kann, weil ihm dort ein Raum offensteht, nennen wir die Freiheit. Das hellblaue Tuch vor dem Fenster nennen wir daher den Schleier der Freiheit.[13]

Hören wir endlich, was dieser Mund sagt. »Schuld und Nichtschuld. Man ist eben so gut oder so schlecht wie man ist. Das Herumdoktern an sich hat wenig Zweck. Man gehe gerade und einfach seinen Weg. Ich halte mich für gut von Natur und sollte ich dann und wann etwas Schlechtes tun, so ist das auch natürlich.«

Diese Sätze hat Paula Modersohn-Becker wirklich geschrieben, in einem Brief, der an ihre Schwester, Milly Rohland-Becker gerichtet war. Er ist datiert vom 12. August 1906, vermutlich ein paar Monate vor dem Bild.[14]

Die Künstlerin wohnte zu dieser Zeit in Paris, begeistert von den jüngsten
Entwicklungen in der Malerei. Sie wollte sich damals von ihrem Manne,
dem deutlich älteren Maler Otto Modersohn trennen, der ihr in der Krise
gleichwohl Unterkunft und Aufenthalt in Paris bezahlte. Die familiäre
Umgebung von Paula konnte ihre Haltung gegenüber dem großzügigen
und geduldigen Gatten nicht begreifen. Sie aber malte und malte.

Was ist ein Bild als Kunstwerk? An welchen Ort gehört es? Was ist ein
Museum? Diese Fragen richten wir an Paula Modersohn-Beckers Selbstbildnis. Dieses Bild nimmt mich in die Bedauer, in die Nähe der portrai-
tierten Person. In dieser Nähe hält es mir den Schleier entgegen, der die
Freiheit offenhält, worin jene Person ist. Das Bild *zeigt* dies alles, es
reicht dies alles dar, es ist reines Sich-Darreichen, das nichts zurück-
hält. Es ist ja nur ein Bild, hat keine Rückseite, verbirgt sich nicht. Das
Bild ist die reine Gabe.

Was gibt das Bild? Es gibt, indem es zeigt, offenlegt, darreicht, das
Sein der Menschin, ihre Freiheit. Aber es ist nur ein Bild. Im Bild ist
kein Sein, nur Schein. Dieses Bild ist also keine echte Gabe, die Malerin
gibt nicht »sich selbst«. So könnte es scheinen. Aber in der Tat ist jedes
echte Geben, nach Lacans Wort, ein Geben dessen, was einer *nicht*
hat, des Nichtseienden.[15] Wie umgekehrt, nach Schellings Satz, das
Nichtseiende im eminenten Sinne nur das Sein selbst ist. Das Sein
aber ist ein Sinn. Die Gabe ist demnach immer Bild; denn das Bild ist
die Sache, insofern sie nicht ist, die Sache als das reine Sich-Geben
des Sinnes.

Wem gibt sich das Bild? – Wohin gehört das Bild? Niemand kann von
sich behaupten, insbesondere der Adressat dieses Bildes zu sein. Dies
könnte auch dann niemand, wenn die Malerin es einer bestimmten Person zugedacht hätte (worüber in diesem Fall nichts bekannt ist). Es ist
auch gar nicht möglich, ein solches Kunstwerk exklusiv irgendwem zu-
zudenken, d. h. andere auszuschließen. Denn dieses Bild ist überhaupt
ein Sich-Zeigen, das, wenn es sich nur überhaupt zeigt, *spricht*; es zeigt
sich aber nur aus dem Abgrund, der ursprünglich Allen gehört, weil vielmehr alle und ein jeder ihm gehören, nämlich aus ihm erst sind, was sie
sind, aus dem Abgrund des Sinnes.

58

Im Körner-Bau hing dieses Selbstbildnis gegenüber der Treppe, die ins Obergeschoß führte, links neben dem Durchgang in eine Reihe von Sälen, die um den Binnenhof gruppiert waren (Abb. S. 24 – 26). Studiert man den Plan des Körner-Baus genauer, so wird man bald gewahr, dass er einen bestimmten Typus Haus inszeniert. Nach dem repräsentativen Eingang mit Ehrenhof kam zunächst eine enge Eingangspassage an der Kasse vorbei. Auf die ein großzügiger Saal folgte, mit Fenstern auf den Ehrenhof, der Empfangssaal. Von hier ging es linker Hand in das »Allerheiligste« des Museums, wo der altdeutsche romanische Adler ausgestellt war – im Hintergrund stand zentral eine spätmittelalterliche Madonnenstatue, gewissermaßen im »Chorschluß« des Saales, der »liebevollen Umbauung des einzelnen Kunstwerkes«, um es mit des Architekten Körner eigenem Wort zu sagen.[16] Geradeaus aber ging es, über ein paar Treppenstufen, zum Minnebrunnen, der in einem eigens für ihn konzipierten Rundsaal stand. Erst nach dem Durchgang durch diesen initiatorischen Raum, gelangte man in den eigentlich »privaten« Bereich des Hauses, der mit dem hier fotografierten Ambiente begann. Es folgte zunächst eine Reihe größerer Säle, dann kleinere und zuletzt das Obergeschoß. Was mit diesem »privaten« Charakter gemeint sei, könnte man kurz wie folgt ausdrücken: Dieses Haus wirkt bewohnt. Allein, der darin wohnt, ist nicht mehr da. Die Gegenstände sind »geschmackvoll« angeordnet, man hat Bezüge hergestellt; der Bodhisattva hat einen zentralen Platz als Hausherr; Paula Modersohn-Becker dagegen (und gegenüber eine orientalische Frauenstatue, die Dienerin, Abb. S. 24 – 25) sind am Eingang zum hinteren Bereich des Hauses, wohin die Frau gehört. Dass genau an der Stelle, die aus dem Gemälde als der Ort des »Brandes« gekennzeichnet ist, ein phallisches Objekt[17] aufgestellt worden, ist ein Lapsus, der zum besseren Verständnis des Bildes nichts, jedoch zum symptomatischen Gehalt dieser Sammlungspräsentation viel beiträgt. Der Fotograf hat dieses Objekt im älteren Foto unmittelbar über der Vitrine des meditierenden Bodhisattva herausragen, im späteren aber, das aus einem tieferen Standpunkt aufgenommen ist, von der Oberseite derselben Vitrine abschneiden lassen. Die Kunstwerke werden durch ihre Aufstellung zu Symbolen der Funktionen des Hauses, mit denen sie, soviel an ihnen selbst liegt, nichts zu tun haben; z. B. hat Paula Modersohn-Beckers Bild offensichtlich ein durchaus gespanntes Verhältnis zu der Funktion, in der es als Symbol, d. h. ertötet,

auftritt. Auch deshalb stehen die Statuen auf Sockeln[18] und in Vitrinen, damit sie zu raumlosen, d. h. abstrakten Signifikanten geworden jene symbolische Funktion übernehmen können. Es ist aber für das Museum wesentlich, dass der Bewohner des Hauses, der die imaginierte Mitte jener symbolischen Funktionen bildet, nicht mehr da, dass er verstorben ist. Das Museum ist insofern ein Grab. Im Falle des Museum Folkwang trägt dieser Verstorbene einen Namen: Karl Ernst Osthaus. Dieser Verstorbene erscheint als eine Form der Entfremdung von Besucher und Objekt. Unser Verhältnis zu den Objekten ist vermittelt durch das jenes verstorbenen Rezipienten, der sie in anderer Weise als das bezahlende Publikum genießen durfte, nämlich als rechtmäßiger Besitzer. Die Entrichtung des Eintrittspreises selbst und die enge Passage vor der Kasse, die den Übergang vom Ehrenhof zum Eingangssaal unterbricht,

ist das Siegel dieser Situation.

Gehen wir nun die Fotografien durch, die Renger-Patzsch von der Sammlung angefertigt hat, so können diese unschwer in zwei Kategorien unterteilt werden: Die einen Bilder zeigen die Werke in situ im Körner-Bau, die anderen zeigen sie einzeln an unbestimmtem Ort. Darunter befinden sich einige auch künstlerisch sehr ansprechende Bilder von alten Vasen und Objekten, teils gruppiert, teils einzeln, aus denen ein anderes Empfinden spricht. Hier gelingt es dem Fotografen, die Einfachheit ihrer dinglichen Existenz im Bild einzufangen, also eine Nähe herzustellen, die dem Besucher des Museums nur schwer zugänglich werden konnte. Dieser Blick ist eigentlich der des Sammlers selbst, dessen, der bei den Objekten wohnt.[19] Der Fotograf hinterbringt diesen Blick dem Publikum und beweist damit den (vermeintlichen) Gehalt an Geheimnis und Wahrheit der Objekte, den sie im mumifizierten Zustand ihrer Präsentation im Museum nicht mehr entfalten können. Die einfache Tatsache, dass der Kunstwert jener Objekte sich in gewisser Hinsicht erst im Bild manifestiert, zeigt selbstverständlich schon an, bis zu welchem Grade dieser im wahrsten Sinne des Wortes imaginär, d. h. eine Funktion des Bildes geworden ist. Dies ändert freilich nichts daran, dass die Objekte selbst wirkliche Kunstwerke sein können, die hier an ihrem eigenen Platze nicht sind. Welcher wäre aber »ihr eigener Platz«? – Das Museum, aber nicht, insofern es ihnen einen Ort gibt, sondern vielmehr,

insofern sie im Museum sich diesen selbst geben.

60

1 Georg Wilhelm Friedrich Hegel, *Phänomenologie des Geistes*, Bamberg und Würzburg 1807, S. 703–704.

2 Ebd. S. 704.

3 Ary Scheffer, *Christi Versuchung*, 1851–57, Paris, Louvre; Paul Gauguin, *Woher kommen wir?, was sind wir?, wohin gehen wir?*, 1897, Boston, Museum of Fine Arts.

4 Thierry de Duve, *Kant after Duchamp*, Boston, Mass. 1998.

5 Roland Barthes, »La mort de l'auteur« (1968), in: Ders., *Œuvres complètes*, Bd. 2, *1966–1973*, hrsg. von Eric Marty, Paris 1994, S. 491–495.

6 Ebd. S. 494.

7 Ebd. S. 492.

8 Ausstellung an der Galerie Franco Noero in Turin, Mai 2006

9 Katalog der Ausstellung *Simon Starling*, Villa Arson, Nizza, und Städtische Ausstellungshalle am Haverkamp, Münster, Münster und Nizza 2004.

10 Jean-Jacques Rousseau beginnt die Konfessionen mit den Sätzen: »Ich beginne ein Unternehmen ohne Beispiel und dessen Ausführung ohne Nachahmung bleiben wird. Ich möchte meinen Nächsten einen Menschen zeigen in der ganzen Wahrheit seiner Natur: Und dieser Mensch werde ich sein.« Rousseau behandelt sich selbst, vielleicht in der Tat zum ersten Mal in der Geschichte der Menschheit, sogar wo er in der ersten Person und für sich selbst spricht – was er die ganze Zeit tut – wie eine dritte Person, die vor einem Gericht, vor Begutachtern steht, als Symptom, insofern sich an seinem Text *zeigen* soll, wer er ist, ohne dass er dies selbst geradewegs *sagen* würde.

11 Siehe z. B. Jean-Marie Scheffer, der es mit der gesamten von ihm so benannten spekulativen Kunsttheorie aufnehmen zu können meint (*L'art de l'âge moderne. L'esthétique et la philosophie de l'art du XVIIIe siècle à nos jours*, Paris 1992), und Yves Michaud, *La crise de l'art contemporain: utopie, démocratie et comédie*, Paris 1997.

12 Daniel Kurjakovic hat einige der Mittel beschrieben, durch die Starling das Ereignis zustande bringt. Siehe »Hide and Seek in Simon Starling's Scenarios«, in: *Simon Starling: Cuttings*, Ausst.-Kat. Kunstmuseum Basel, Museum für Gegenwartskunst, und Power Plant, Toronto, Basel 2005, S. C26–C36.

13 »Die Freiheit ist das lichtend Verbergende, in dessen Lichtung jener Schleier weht, der das Wesende aller Wahrheit verhüllt und den Schleier als den verhüllenden erscheinen lässt.« Martin Heidegger, »Die Frage nach der Technik«, in: Ders., *Vorträge und Aufsätze*, Stuttgart [10]2004 (1954), S. 29.

14 *Paula Modersohn-Becker in Briefen und Tagebüchern*, hrsg. von Günter Busch und Liselotte von Reinken, Frankfurt a. M. 1979, S. 456.

15 »Ce qui est aimé dans l'objet, c'est ce dont il manque – on ne donne que ce qu'on n'a pas.« Jacques Lacan, *Le séminaire, livre IV*, hrsg. von Jacques-Alain Miller, Paris 1994, S. 151.

16 Zitiert nach *Essener Allgemeine Zeitung* vom 5. Mai 1929.

17 Inventarisiert als Löwe, frühorientalisch, Bronze, Inv. K 536.

18 Das »Problem« des Sockels im Sinne eines Manzoni oder Rückriem entsteht überhaupt erst unter solchen Umständen.

19 Osthaus hat schon selbst seine Sammlung der Öffentlichkeit zugänglich gemacht und in seiner Museumsgründung eine wesentliche Aufgabe gesehen. Der Hagener Museumsbau, worin seine Sammlung zuerst untergebracht war, wäre eigens zu analysieren, besitzt jedoch auch im allgemeinen ebenfalls einen »privaten« Charakter.

Albert Renger-Patzsch

1897	wird am 22. Juni in Würzburg geboren; der Vater, Musikalien- und Buchhändler von Beruf, ist begeisterter Amateurfotograf
1909–16	sammelt erste praktische Erfahrungen mit der Fotografie und technische Erkenntnisse
1916–18	Militärdienst im Ersten Weltkrieg
1919	beginnt ein Chemiestudium an der Technischen Hochschule in Dresden
1920	übernimmt die Leitung des Bildarchivs in dem von Ernst Fuhrmann geleiteten Folkwang-Verlag in Hagen, fotografiert für die von Fuhrmann herausgegebenen Bücher in europäischen Museen
1922	Umzug nach Darmstadt, erste Pflanzen- und Tieraufnahmen
1923	verlässt den Folkwang-Verlag, arbeitet für eine Pressebildagentur in Berlin und als Buchhalter
1924	setzt die Zusammenarbeit mit Ernst Fuhrmann in dessen neugeründetem Auriga-Verlag fort
1925	Umzug nach Bad Harzburg, Eröffnung eines Ateliers; Veröffentlichung seines ersten Buchs *Das Chorgestühl von Cappenberg*
1926	wird Mitglied des Deutschen Werkbundes
1927	lernt Carl Georg Heise, Direktor des Museums für Kunst und Kulturgeschichte der Hansestadt Lübeck kennen, der im Dezember die erste umfangreiche Einzelausstellung des Fotografen im Behnhaus in Lübeck organisiert; in den folgenden Jahren Veröffentlichung einer Reihe von Büchern, diverse Einzelausstellungen sowie Teilnahme an wichtigen internationalen Fotoausstellungen
1929	siedelt nach Essen über, fotografiert den Museumsbestand im Museum Folkwang für dessen Archiv; Stadtlandschaften und Industrieaufnahmen des Ruhrgebiets werden zu seinen bevorzugten Motiven
1933	wird zum 1. Oktober als Leiter der Fachabteilung *Bildmäßige Fotografie* an die Folkwangschule für Gestaltung berufen, lässt seinen Vertrag vor Beginn des zweiten Semesters auslaufen
1935	Ausstellung in The Royal Photographic Society of Great Britain, London
1941–43	wird nach einem halben Jahr Kriegsdienst freigestellt; Kriegsberichterstatter für die Organisation Todt
1944	ein Großteil seines Archivs im Museum Folkwang (18.000 Negative) wird durch einen Bombenangriff zerstört; siedelt mit seiner Familie nach Wameln am Möhnesee bei Soest über
1960	Verleihung des Kulturpreises der Deutschen Gesellschaft für Photographie
1964	wird Mitglied der Gesellschaft Deutscher Lichtbildner
1965	erhält einen Staatspreis des Kunsthandwerks vom Land Nordrhein-Westfalen
1966	stirbt am 27. September in Wameln; am 21. Dezember wird die von Otto Steinert organisierte Ausstellung *Albert Renger-Patzsch: Der Fotograf der Dinge* im Ruhrland- und Heimatmuseum, Essen, eröffnet.

Im Museum Folkwang werden in den Jahren 1928, 1929, 1931 und 1940 Arbeiten von Albert Renger-Patzsch ausgestellt.

Simon Starling

Geb. 1967 in Epsom, Surrey, GB, lebt und arbeitet in Kopenhagen, Berlin und Glasgow. Studium an der Glasgow School of Art. Zwischen 1990–96 arbeitet er hauptsächlich als Fotograf für Museen und Galerien in Schottland. Ausstellungen u. a. am Moderna Museet, Stockholm, The Modern Institute, Glasgow, Camden Arts Centre, London, Fundació Joan Miró, Barcelona, Museum für Gegenwartskunst, Basel. Gewinner des renommierten Turner Prize 2005.

Bruno Haas

Geb. 1967, Studium der Kunstgeschichte und Philosophie in Bonn, Freiburg, Paris, Rom. Publikationen zur Philosophie des deutschen Idealismus, zur Methodologie (»deiktisch-funktionale Analyse«) und zur Kunstgeschichte von der Renaissance bis zur Gegenwart. Maître de Conférences an der Sorbonne, Paris 1.

Werke des Museum Folkwang im Nachbau von Simon Starling

Farbige Reproduktion
Giorgio de Chirico Abb. S. 30, 31
Selbstbildnis mit Palette, 1924
Tempera auf Leinwand, 76 x 61 cm, bez. u. l.: G. de Chirico se ipsum pinxit 1924
Erworben 1927, beschlagnahmt 1937, jetzt Kunstmuseum Winterthur, Geschenk der
Gebrüder Sulzer AG zum 125jährigen Bestehen der Firma, 1959

Farbige Reproduktion
Erich Heckel Abb. S. 25
Genesende (Triptychon), 1912–1913
Öl auf Leinwand, 98,7 x 244,8 cm
Erworben 1930, beschlagnahmt 1937, jetzt Busch-Reisinger Museum,
Harvard University Art Museums, Edmée Busch Greenough Fund, Harvard

Aristide Maillol Abb. S. 30
Der Radrennfahrer, 1907/08
Bronze, 98 x 30 x 20 cm, bez. auf dem Sockel: AM, Gießerstempel: Cire Valsuani Paris
Erworben vor 1912 Inv. P 36

Farbige Reproduktion
Franz Marc Abb. S. 25
Rote Pferde, 1911
Öl auf Leinwand, 121 x 183 cm
Erworben 1911, beschlagnahmt 1937, jetzt Privatsammlung, Dauerleihgabe im
Busch-Reisinger Museum, Harvard University Art Museums, Harvard

Paula Modersohn-Becker Abb. S. 24, 26
Selbstbildnis mit Kamelienzweig, 1906/07
Öl auf Holz, 61,5 x 30,5 cm, bez. u. l.: P M B.
Erworben 1918, beschlagnahmt 1937, rückerworben 1957 Inv. G 269

Farbige Reproduktion
Otto Mueller Abb. S. 24, 30, 33
Akte im Dickicht, 1915
Leimfarbe auf Rupfen, 85,6 x 100 cm
Erworben vor 1929, beschlagnahmt 1937, jetzt Westfälisches Landesmuseum
für Kunst und Kulturgeschichte, Münster

Emil Nolde Abb. S. 24, 26, 30
Stilleben mit Holzfigur, 1911
Öl auf Leinwand, 77 x 65 cm, bez. auf dem Keilrahmen: Emil Nolde Stilleben
Erworben 1911, beschlagnahmt 1937, rückerworben 1994 Inv. G 527

Schwarzer Fels mit Wasserrosen und Schnecke (Senfkorngarten) Abb. S. 29
Farbiger Holzschnitt auf Japanpapier, 31,7 x 24,6 cm
Erworben 1927 Inv. A 2/07

Schwarzgraue Felsform mit grünem Moos (Zehnbambushalle) Abb. S. 29
Farbiger Holzschnitt auf Japanpapier, 28,2 x 25,2 cm
Erworben 1927 Inv. A 3/07

Korinthische Kanne mit Kleeblattmündung, Fälschung, um 1890 Abb. S. 30
Ton, H. 50 cm, Durchmesser 28,3 cm
Erworben vor 1921 Inv. A 7

Großes Vasengefäß mit Rosettenauflage, China, 6. Jh. Abb. S. 26
Ton, grüne Glasur, H. 41,2 cm, Durchmesser 35 cm Inv. K 242

Vase, China Abb. S. 30
Gebrannter Ton, H. 24,5 cm, Durchmesser 34,5 cm Inv. K 243

Yangshao Vase, China (2200 – 1700 v. Chr.) Abb. S. 25, 29
Urnengefäß, Irdenware, 36,8 x 37 x 34 cm
Erworben 1926 Inv. K 268

Dame, China, späte Tang-Zeit (618 – 906) Abb. S. 29
Weißlicher Ton, 27,5 x 7,9 x 6,5 cm Inv. K 313

Große Vase nach Metallvorbild, China, Han (206 v. Chr. – 220 n. Chr.) Abb. S. 30
Ton, H. 18,2 cm, Durchmesser 33 cm Inv. K 337

Vogel, China, Han (206 v. Chr. – 220 n. Chr.) Abb. S. 29
Ton, gelbgrüne Glasur, 14,6 x 7,8 x 13 cm, Ständer 1,6 x 8 x 8 cm Inv. K 359

Liegender Hund, China, Wei (386 – 524) Abb. S. 29
Ton, Kreidebemalung rötlich, 12,4 x 18,8 x 12,2 cm
Erworben 1929 Inv. K 360

Schauspieler, China, Tang (618 – 906) Abb. S. 29
Gebrannter Ton, Reste alter Bemalung, 27,2 x 11,5 x 11,8 cm
Erworben 1927 Inv. K 361

Weltenwächter, China, Tang (618 – 906) Abb. S. 29
Gebrannter Ton, rötlicher Scherben, mit Sockel 57 x 19,5 x 8,5 cm
Erworben 1927 Inv. K 382

Löwe, frühorientalisch Abb. S. 26
Bronze, 22,7 x 9,9 x 18,5 cm
Erworben vor 1921 Inv. K 536

Wandbehang, Tibet, um 1680 – 1720 Abb. S. 24
Wolle, 200 x 122 cm Inv. K 716

Kundlka, Korea, Koryŏ-Dynastie (935 – 1392), 11. Jh. Abb. S. 26
Bronze, 27,8 x 12,5 x 11 cm Inv. K 717

Kleine Priesterfigur auf Lotosblüte, China, Tang (618 – 907) Abb. S. 26
Bronze, 6,5 x 1,7 x 1,6 cm Inv. KPL 51

Kopf eines Buddha, Japan Abb. S. 29
Bronze, 7,8 x 6,6 x 6,6 cm
Erworben vor 1921 Inv. KPL 49